# PERMISSION TO LAND

Caitlin Press Inc.
3375 Ponderosa Way
Qualicum Beach, BC V9K 2J8
www.caitlinpress.com

Text and cover design by Vici Johnstone
Cover photo Alphonse LeBlanc
Family tree illustrated by Brian Latta

Edited by Pam Robertson
Printed in Canada

Caitlin Press Inc. acknowledges financial support from the Government of Canada and the Canada Council for the Arts, and the Province of British Columbia through the British Columbia Arts Council and the Book Publisher's Tax Credit.

Library and Archives Canada Cataloguing in Publication

Permission to land : a memoir of loss, discovery and identity /
Judy LeBlanc.
LeBlanc, Judy, author.
Canadiana 20230522653 | ISBN 9781773861357 (softcover)
LCSH: LeBlanc, Judy. | LCSH: LeBlanc, Judy—Family. | LCSH: Racially mixed families—
British Columbia. | LCSH: British Columbia—Biography. | CSH: Coast Salish—British Columbia. |
CSH: Coast Salish—Ethnic identity. | LCGFT: Autobiographies.
LCC E99.S21 L43 2024 | DDC 971.1004/97940092—dc23

# Permission to Land

A Memoir of Loss, Discovery and Identity

## Judy LeBlanc

CAITLIN PRESS 2024

for Mom, in loving memory

*Sometimes the end is told before the beginning.*
*One must walk backwards on footprints*
*that walked forward*
*for the story to be told.*

*I will try this backward walk.*

—Louise B. Halfe, Sky Dancer, from
"āniskōstēw – connecting"
in *Burning in This Midnight Dream*

# Contents

# I'd Like to Acknowledge That

I would like to lean on the edge of what I know. I would like to lean on a ledge and gnaw on the blank bone of history, to map the rivers of the body's tissue. Connect at the confluence. I would like to act. To act, to gnaw and know. I would like to act knowledge. I would like to acknowledge.

I would like to acknowledge I'm on. Let's say OM. In which the only I is the third. Can you hear the vibration? It's in the sea that surrounds this I land. In the drumbeat and the bagpipe. Wind high in cedar branch. I'd like to acknowledge OM, meaning me and my Scottish great-great-grandfather and my Salish great-great-grandmother and all those before and after we, and the sea and cedar, fir and salal and all that grows and breathes, and urban strut and street and vibe. We would like to acknowledge I'm. I am. Here now.

I'd like to cede that I'm acknowledged and you're not. I'd like to acknowledge that I've unseated you, treated you amiss and deleted you. I'd like to add knowledge to the terror story. Great Great Grandma married Hudson's Bay Man and tainted her blood with Euro spam. Wife of the country, womb of the country, from which sprung mothers and sisters and me.

I'd like to acknowledge that I'm on the unceded terror and that I am the unceded terror. Fur and coal and fish and timber. I have a house in a thin-rooted wood above a rising sea. Late at night the vibration of the Pentlatch voices in their tongue thrum like ghosts through my open windows. Drumbeat. Someday the cedars will fall on my roof because of long droughts and tenuous roots. I am a beneficiary of this stinking thievery. I'd like to cede you. I'd like to see you.

# FROM WHO I AM BORN

I can trace my Coast Salish ancestors on my mother's side back to 1853 when a woman named ZIȼOT of the W̱SÁNEĆ Nation married a Scot named Peter Bartleman. Their daughter Rosalie married William Houston, whose mother came from either the Suquamish tribe in Washington or the Tsleil-Waututh Nation from Burrard Inlet in British Columbia. Rosalie and William were my great-grandparents. Their oldest of eight children was my great-aunt Stella, and their youngest was my grandmother, who had six children including my mother.

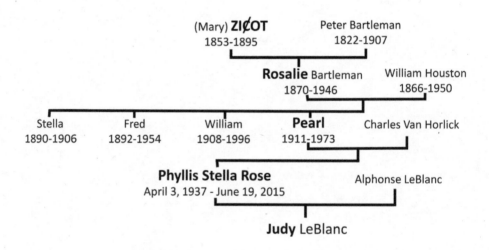

# FAMILY TREE

My mother was named *Phyllis Stella Rose*. She went by Rose, recalling the wildflower, its petals that tear, its thorns. She had a quick smile for the camera, a coquettish tilt of the chin. I've been going through boxes of family photos. Most are arranged neatly in albums while others are in Ziploc bags awaiting my mother's prowess for organization, a chore she will never complete.

After my mother died, I saw that she wasn't fixed in my history but lived on in my body's tics and follicles, my DNA, the image of myself in the mirror. She inhabited my dreams and lingered in photographs where she's at the mercy of the camera's shutter and the gaze of the living. I want to go back in time, to ask the questions I never asked: about this history she's left me, of which I know so little, to probe the silences, and to understand what it means to acknowledge an ancestry without claiming an identity. Who were her Coast Salish grandmothers, and therefore mine? What did they mean to her and what do they mean to me? Which is the longest reach, from present to past or from past to present? Finally, the only possible route is from known to unknown.

## i) Rose, June 12, 2011

In the photo a woman in her early seventies wears a straw hat, and through the tiny holes in its weave the sunlight makes a pattern of circles forming a corona around her head. Her eyes are concealed behind thin-rimmed glasses, and a hesitant smile plays around her mouth. Behind her, the lake bleaches blue to white, and the mountains in the far distance are a greenish blur. In the brightness of the summer day and the wash of light, there's a porousness to the image that is unsettling. The woman is my mother, and she will die in four years and eight days.

I was with her both days, the day she died and the day this photo was taken by my husband. Also present outside the frame of the photo were my father, my daughter and her husband, my mother's sister and brother. We were on our way from the West Coast to my niece's wedding in Canmore, Alberta, and had stopped in Kelowna to pick up my uncle from the care home and take him out for lunch. None of us are in the photo, all us family members. It's my mother only, she who so often was surrounded by others, as if she's on a solitary journey and merely smiling into the day.

Even if I know she's not alone, looking at the photo, I'm able to imagine that my mother could be another woman, one she must have dreamed of in her most private moments. This woman of my imagination sits enjoying a glass of wine on a lakeshore in a wide-brimmed hat in a tourist town in the interior. She's free of the encumbrances of family or history. Did my mother ever wonder what it might have been like to live a life other than the one she lived? Now that I'm older, and now that she's gone, I sometimes wonder this myself. Not that there's anything extraordinary in my fantasy, only that it might have been different in small ways, and maybe some large. Now that she's dead, and I'm nearing the age she is in the photo, I'm able to imagine her wondering, for example, what it might have been like had she not had me. I'm now able to hold that thought and know that it wouldn't have meant she didn't love me in the best way she could, which is what we do.

The photo sits on my desk, and some days I want to shake my mother from her inertia, pull her into the present and protect her from all that I know is coming, or is it to protect me from losing her for good? How many ways you lose your mother throughout a life, starting from when you're taken from her body as an infant. For good, we say, to describe what we think of as that final losing.

## ii) Rose, Mid-1960s

In the photo the house is cut off at the attic. This is how my mother lived her life, or tried to, as if there was no attic. The house pushes its bay window outward like a chest wanting a medal. My mother stands beneath the window in front of a flower garden bordered with rock. She saw beauty in flowers and in the geometry of houses: cathedral entrances and dormer windows, slant of light. This isn't to say she didn't have practical considerations: size, modernity, the neighbourhood. My father was the same, only for him the attraction wasn't aesthetic so much as a dream of prestige at a time when home ownership was the only definition of success for the postwar working class.

The door up the front steps is in shadow on the covered porch.

Once there was a knock at that front door and my older brother answered.

"Is your father here?" the man asked.

My brother, who might have been twelve at the time, replied, "He doesn't live here anymore."

The man went away. I, who would have been eleven at the time, said to my brother, "You're not supposed to tell anyone that." My brother and I stood for a moment at the closed door in silence, he wide-eyed while I stood frozen with shame seeding somewhere inside of me because my mother was alone with four children.

After a year, my father came back. One time—I don't remember if it was before he moved out or after he moved back in—he drove his Volkswagen bug in mad circles on the front lawn while my mother screamed at him from the porch to stop. I coaxed her into the house and made her a cup of tea.

There is a madness in attics, but the attic doesn't exist in this photo.

She's in her twenties or early thirties—how do I know? A flirty fist on hip, knees slightly bent, and her slender body draws the eye to her physicality. White slacks end above her delicate brown ankles. The summer sun illuminates the living room window behind her. White sheers are visible. There's no seeing in. Her hair is a shock of raven black against this radiance.

My mother squints into the camera and is not exactly smiling. She could be described as petite, but there's a force within her. If you turn the photo, the tilt is of no consequence. Always, she will hold fast.

In his effort to capture both the house and the entirety of my mother's body, my father has stood too far back. Between him and my mother is a ribbon of grey hardpan, a small section of the circular drive on which she stands. I wonder which of his possessions he's most keen to forefront. Neither the house nor my mother submit easily to ownership.

## iii) Women, December 1968

The four of us representing three generations are wedged together on the couch: my mother with my six-year-old sister on her lap, then Grandma Pearl, and me beside her. My twelve-year-old body is cut off from the shoulders down, my eyes are lowered and I lean forward as if about to bolt. My little sister slants toward the photo's frame. None of us want to be there.

A string of pearls accents the red dress that flatters my mother's tiny figure and contrasts elegantly with her coifed black hair. She's dressed up for this occasion, my grandmother's visit. It's Christmas, and she's cleaned and baked for two weeks after her shifts at the grocery store. Her mouth is more brightly lipsticked than her mother's, though both women have similar expressions on their face: tight jaw muscles and a slight effort at a smile. Grandma Pearl, wearing a white cardigan and a skirt not quite long enough to hide her stubby knees, has squared her shoulders to the camera. The direction of her gaze is toward my father, who's taking the picture, though the rhinestones on her glasses deflect the light and conceal her eyes. She fully occupies the centre of the photo, her posture broadcasting a mix of wariness and defiance. My mother will one day adopt this stance, and so will I.

My mother tilts her head toward my grandmother with her shoulder torqued in the opposite direction. It's the tension in this opposition that touches me the most: the daughter, despite herself, poised as if wanting to rest her head on her mother's shoulder.

### iv) Grandma Pearl, Late 1950s

Her name, Pearl, suggests something white and hard, born of agitation. She started life out as a Houston, her father's name, which absorbed the one attached to her mother: Bartleman. Her first married name was Van Horlick, and all her children, including my mother, are Van Horlicks. After the divorce there was a man who beat her and the children then left, but she didn't take his name. Finally, Van Horlick was absorbed by a new husband and she became a McKee.

The photo is black and white, overexposed, so that its shadows are dense and its bright spots luminescent. In the foreground Grandma Pearl and her husband Howard McKee are dwarfed by darkness behind and above them except where traces of dappled sunlight reveal the trees of a forest. They sit at a table covered with a white cloth and various dishes, coffee cups, a jug of milk or maybe orange juice. Howard is in shade though a patch of sunshine highlights the jaunty white cap on his head, the hat I imagine my grandmother asked him to wear. "Wear this, Hon, it suits you." It was said he was *a good man*, that finally Pearl had a good man. My grandmother, whose hair was naturally as straight as my mother's, would have curled her hair for this lunch out at the edge of the forest.

She and Howard face forward, his mouth in a perfect O as if caught in mid-sentence. Both surprised by the shutter of the camera. Grandma is much shorter than her husband, and her shoulders are slightly hunched, her eyes squinting, while her face and body are bleached white from the full sun that washes over her. In this abundance of light against the dark background she can't see what I see, her elfin face and black curls, her own shininess.

### v) Pearl, About 1940

In this, one of only three photos I have of Grandmother Pearl, I'm surprised at her youthfulness, her small stature. In her twenties, she's already a mother of four, with four more to come. If I stare long enough, it's as if I hear her thoughts, her voice, and I know her in a way I never knew her in life.

Though Pearl's brother-in-law is a tall glass of water like her husband, it's not him but her mother she longs to stand next to. As always, her mother, Rosalie, is propped up by Pearl's brother Fred way down on the other end of the line in this family photo. Always, since Stella, her sister, died, or so Pearl is told. Pearl is the youngest in the family and wasn't even around in 1906 when this sister she never met, the oldest in the family, died. Never mind, it was five years before Pearl was born. It was as if when Pearl opened her infant mouth for the first time to cry out in hunger, in the shadowy corner of the room hovered Stella.

Mother and daughter abut either end of the photo, a round-faced smiling Rosalie angled toward her tall son who rests his arm on her shoulder, and Pearl only half there, not smiling. A quarter of Pearl's body is shaved off where she stands behind her brother-in-law's elbow. Her mouth is curved into a frown and her arms are crossed. She's a skinny petite thing with straight black hair, Charlie Van Horlick's scrawny dark-eyed wife.

In the middle of the photo, all three of the towering men and the broad-shouldered blonde woman are smiling.

Look at Charlie now, lips puckered around a dangling cigarette, his arm snugging the big blonde what's-her-name close, and Pearl and Charlie's boy and girl at their feet like they belong to Blondie. Pearl can smell Charlie's whiskey breath from where she stands. Didn't her mom warn her about him, though her dad said Charlie would take care of their little Pearl, that he was a *worker*, that he came from a big respectable family who owned a ranch.

Oh, her Charlie, for better or worse, is a smooth-talking hunk of man, and even her mom says they make beautiful children together. Just look at her little boy; was there ever a more handsome child, that sweet shy pout on his face? And Rosie, her China doll, sticking her chest out proud as can be and staring straight at the camera with that scowl and those piercing eyes. Didn't Pearl holler at her to stop scowling and Charlie bark back without taking his eyes off Blondie, "Leave her alone, Pearl."

Had Stella lived she would have loved Pearl; Pearl just knows it. Her big sister, Stella, would have been twenty-one when Pearl was born, and she would have sung her the songs their mother Rosalie sang to Stella when she was a baby, songs Rosalie stopped singing before Pearl was born, the old songs her Bartleman grandmother sang in their language, a language Pearl will never know. Stella would have braided her little sister's hair and taken her to pick buckets of berries in the summer.

Almost eighty years later, Pearl's granddaughter will wonder if her own mother, who is little Rosie of the scowl, ever saw this photo. She'll ask her uncle, who's still handsome at eighty-five, about the blonde. Her uncle, who since his sister's death misses her phone calls, will shrug his shoulders. Though the uncle and the granddaughter know, Pearl in the photo doesn't yet know that she'll one day leave Charlie.

Little Rosie doesn't know and will never know that in her middle name she carries the ghost of the oldest sister who died: *Stella*. Or perhaps she knew all along, the way we sometimes know things without being told, or being told but not telling.

## vi) Great-Grandparents' House, Possibly Early 1920s

A small wooden house stands in a clearing in the woods. It's constructed of simple lines, the architecture a child may render in pencil, a setting for a fairy tale. Two narrow windows interrupt the outside wall, the lower one slightly off-centre on the clapboard siding. Not a grand house; there's an ease in the architecture, a modesty. It's of the type built in the early part of the twentieth century. You see them in mining and logging communities. The ghost of a split-rail fence traces the foreground, and the house is centred nicely in the frame. A shadow traces the roof line beneath the eaves, above the broad brush of the sun on the clapboard. My great-grandparents are nowhere to be seen; my grandmother as a little girl and her older brother are nowhere to be seen. The eldest brothers and sisters, except the two who died, have all left home by now. It's as if the house has been deserted despite the curtains in the windows.

This photo is unpeopled and, not necessarily because of that, there is no immediate evidence of what Barthes calls the wound in the photograph, unless the wound is absence, which means there's always a wound. It seems that besides the empty house, the forest behind is full of absence, and yet a forest is never absent of life. I stare at the photo until a tiny opening in the trees high above the house reveals itself and the snout of a bear and its eyes emerge; not a real bear because its size is disproportionate, more like a mirage or a carving on a totem pole.

After the film is developed, my great-grandmother turns the photograph over in her lined and aging hands. She slips her new Waterman fountain pen between her fingers the way the nuns taught her so many years ago, and she writes the following, smiling all the time, feeling that she has come through difficult times to finally be rewarded in, let's say, her fiftieth year. I like to think she imagines a great-granddaughter reading her words one day.

> This is our house
> at Brackendale
>
> 3 large rooms with
> modern plumbing in
> the kitchen—Bathroom

# FROM WHERE I WRITE

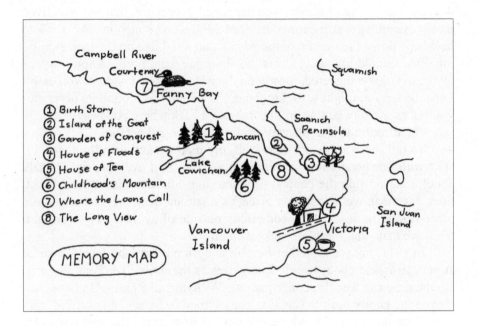

Campbell River
Courtenay
⑦ Fanny Bay
Squamish

① Birth Story
② Island of the Goat
③ Garden of Conquest
④ House of Floods
⑤ House of Tea
⑥ Childhood's Mountain
⑦ Where the Loons Call
⑧ The Long View

Duncan
Saanich Peninsula
Lake Cowichan
Vancouver Island
Victoria
San Juan Island

MEMORY MAP

# MEMORY MAP

## i) Birth Story

I come from Vancouver Island, which sits in the Pacific Ocean and cants toward the broken edge of a vast continent. A topographical map reveals where you might fit its jagged shoreline, as if it were a puzzle, into that of the mainland. *The mainland.* When I was young I believed, and maybe still do, that everything of importance happened over there, that we who lived on the island were somehow outsiders. Mountains bunch up like a raised backbone down the middle of the island, and a red line on the map signifying 19A, the old highway, skirts the shoreline from north to south where all the towns are clustered, mostly on the island's eastern side. If you didn't know better you might walk for about 450 kilometres around its perimeter without ever really getting anywhere except back where you began, though you would return to that place of origin as a changed person.

To tell the origin story of myself, my mothers and grandmothers, I'll start with our geography: *where we are from.* Is it even possible to talk about a life outside the context of where that life took place? And if not, does this mean we belong to a place, as if sprung from the land, or does a place belong to us, as if it's something outside of us that, like a cartographer, we map, and therefore stake a claim?

In 1911, my grandmother Pearl was born on San Juan Island, a small American island about twenty kilometres as the crow flies from Victoria. By the time she was three, her parents, William and Rosalie Houston, had moved the family back to Canada. They settled in Squamish, north of Vancouver on the mainland, where my mother Rose spent the first few years of her life before her parents, Pearl and Charlie Van Horlick, moved the family to Hope, 150 kilometres inland. In her late teens, after her parents' divorce, my mother and my grandmother with her third husband, as well as two of my aunties, made their way to Vancouver Island. Around this time my mother met and married my father in Cowichan Bay.

At the time, Dad worked in logging camps in remote places on the island where sometimes it was possible to bring along his family. According to Auntie, in the summer of 1956 when Mom was pregnant with me, my parents and my oldest brother were housed in a motel near Lake Cowichan, along with other loggers employed by the company. Auntie, who would have been twelve years old, was staying with them to help Mom out. It was a hot summer day, and my mother was nine months pregnant, huge and irritable with the August heat and the boredom. They were far from a decent grocery store, any kind of shopping or entertainment, surrounded on one side by the forest and the other the lonely highway. Bears would have come sniffing around the motel. When her water broke Mom cried out, and with labour fully underway each contraction caused her to double over in pain. In between contractions she paced around the motel room, sweat pooling on her skin, snapping at her youngest sister to "do something." Auntie, young enough to know little about childbirth, described how she flew out the door and hoofed it up the hill to the office, which, the way she tells it, was *at least one hundred miles away. Hoofed* is the word she uses when she tells this story, and she mentions her short legs. She rotates her arms around her compact body as if she's running and imitates breathlessness, though now this is easy as she's on an oxygen tank most of the day. "I yelled at the big boss up at the office, 'You have to come quick, my sister is dying.'" Mom was rushed to the hospital in Duncan, a half-hour away by taxi, and I was born a few hours later. I sometimes ask Auntie to tell the story again because it makes us both laugh. I like to hear how I began my journey into the world on the edge of a forest where bears and cougars roamed, not so far from the sounds of the saws and the stricken mountain-sides; that there was tension as there is with birth, and in the end, there was a story, and also there was laughter.

## ii) Island of the Goat

Brentwood Bay, Saanich Peninsula, near Victoria

In my family we call it *the island* in the way we call Vancouver Island *the island*, as if it belongs to us, so we camp there when we want, which is often, for at least two summers during my childhood, and except for the goat, we're always alone. Just a few years ago, Philip Kevin Paul told me that the island's name in SENĆOŦEN, the language of the Saanich people, is SEN,NI,NES (Senanus), which in English means *chest raised up*. Chest in this context means both *landable* and *where the mind is*. Therefore, *to land* is to know from the heart where you are, to have that bond between heart and place.

The first time I see the goat, I'm about ten years old. Reclined on the yellow grass above the shore, its back legs are curled beneath its body, and its front legs stretched before it as if in a gesture of supplication. A set of grey horns protrudes from its head in a gentle swoop behind him. He's covered in a thick black and white coat, matted and grey in places. On his chest a patch as round and large as a saucer, where the hair has been rubbed raw, exposes the pink flesh beneath. It's as if he's been in a fight or fallen or been chewed by bugs. In my child's mind, it's the flesh that fascinates me, what's beneath his coat, and I assume the goat must be hurting. If not for the horns and the strangeness of his presence, I would step closer and offer comfort. Instead, I kneel on the scratchy grass about three metres away from him. He tilts his heavy head in my direction and fixes old eyes on mine. I return his stare with an uneasy feeling that he's not quite real but more like a ghost.

Partly I want to keep my discovery a secret because I'm afraid the goat will be made too ordinary through the eyes of my family, yet I'm in need of their reassurance that things are as they seem, free of that which isn't easily explained. I leave the goat and return to the little bay where we landed an hour before. The tent is up and our wooden boat, anchored just offshore, rocks in the breeze, my father at the motor, fixing and adjusting. My older brother, who's in the shade reading comics, says he's disappointed that the bear didn't eat me. "There's no bears on the island, Stupid," I say. My mother, younger brother and sister play in the shallow water at the shoreline. When she sees me, my mother says, "You could have helped unload and set up camp before disappearing into the woods," then she wants to slather me in baby oil to keep my skin from drying out in the sun. I don't like comics or baby oil. I prefer to be in the cool of the firs and the giant maples that cover much of the island, or on the shore, where the arbutus with their smooth, red and peeling trunks lean over the water like human limbs, and their ever-falling leaves crackle beneath my feet—so fallible.

My parents know nothing about the goat, though they want to see for themselves. I lead them through the woods to where he lies on the grass exactly as I left him. He raises his old head and looks at my family then blinks his eyes shut. My father suggests that he's been left there to shorten the grass, that someone brings him water. My older brother says he's an evil goat who's been cast out. My mother says the goat is old or lame, and no longer of any use, so has been left to die on the island. My father says if that were the case, its owner would simply have shot him. My little sister calls him Billy Goat Gruff, and my younger brother says a wolf will get him, at which we all laugh and say, "There are no wolves on the island." All we know for sure is there it is—a goat alone on an island in the middle of Brentwood Bay.

..

Philip Kevin Paul described an additional meaning for *chest* as *pain*. When I was a child, we knew no SENĆOŦEN words, but we knew that the island was an ancient burial ground for the local First Nations people. How we knew this, I don't know. Most likely my father heard it from someone at the marina, someone he considered *in the know*: a fisherman, a man with a large boat. How many children were buried on the island? How much tragedy beneath its benign grassy meadow, the goat's belly?

Despite the island's history as a gravesite, I don't recall any signs warning us away, let alone discussion about the rightness of our presence there. The past and the dead were of no consequence to my family. I'd always known my mother had relations on the reserve—I thought of them then as related to her, not to me or my siblings—but this was not something we talked about. My mother concerned herself only with whatever the next hour, day and week would demand of her. My father maintained that the past is past and didn't bear mentioning.

SEN,NI,NES wasn't our island, nor was it *the* island, as if there were no others. It has belonged to the W̱SÁNEĆ people for thousands of years, but during my childhood we didn't call the First Nations across the water by their SENĆOŦEN name, nor did we call them First Nations. We called them the "Indians on the reserve." The reserve we were speaking of is Tsartlip, or W̱JOȽEȽP, meaning in English *where the maples grow*. Even though my great-grandmother came from W̱JOȽEȽP, this isn't knowledge that has been passed down to me. I know it only because I've googled Saanich place names, which led me to Dave Elliott Senior's book *Saltwater People*.

It's as if the goat wants to pass something on to me, and I stare into its old eyes looking for a clue. In my child's mind, the goat has been there since the beginning of time, and some days after my visit to him, I sit on the swollen stone above the shore beneath the leaning arbutus. I stare across the water to the other side, to where the *Indians* live, who I also believe have been there since the beginning of time. My own life seems so transitory, the way I flit with my family from the island to home and back again, all the time chattering and arguing like the gulls. Beside the goat, how foolish my family seems. I imagine my great-grandmother across the bay, like me, scrambling over the mossy rocks along the shore. Did she also encounter the goat, there on the other side where he might have once lived?

In her later years, I asked my mother about her grandmother, and she said she remembered nothing. And yet, after my mother died, my sister gave me a document written by my mother for my nephew when he did a high school project about his family. In her neat and careful script, she writes that her grandmother, who *always had a hug for her*, once bought her a dress. *Pink taffeta with a bow at the back. Taffeta* is underlined. She goes on to say that she was *very proud of that dress*. To retain this level of detail, my mother would have had to revisit the memory several times, possibly even revise it. Did the act of writing allow her into the past she otherwise refused, or was it always there, that taffeta dress, cradled lovingly in the folds of her mind? My mother grew to love the aesthetics of a well-chosen dress. I want to attribute it to the memory of a grandmother's gift, but I know it's possible my mother, who turned her back on her people across the water, liked the idea of a taffeta dress because to her it represented a world of privilege.

We never learned of the goat's origins. I can't help but think he remains on that island, to which I've never returned except in my mind. I see

Senanus when I cross the Malahat on my way to Victoria. On a clear day, it appears to heave its proud chest above the surface of the water. My mother, who believed in guardian spirits, often told me my grandfather, long dead, watched over me. Though she never said so, did she believe her grand-mother, who always had a hug for her and that very special gift of a taffeta dress, was her guardian spirit? I now know that my great-grandmother died when my mother was ten years old, the age I was that first summer on the island. My mother and my grandmother, who I barely knew, never spoke of my great-grandmother, and yet those days on the island I missed her, the great-grandmother I never met and knew not at all.

### iii) Garden of Conquest

Saanich, near Victoria

Not interested in flowers. That's not why we went. I was interested in a boy, and we were high. Late 1970s, that's what you did, or what I did, although I now know there were others, more serious, who were getting on with their lives. I was flittering between entry-level jobs and couch surfing. Yes, I have my regrets. From the little I remember about the boy he was slender and maybe two years older than me. I was eighteen. He drove a Volkswagen van, not a Westfalia like I would own several years later, after reading about them in the *Lemon-Aid* guide: their high rating on storage efficiency despite being low on engine efficiency. I was inter-ested in storage because post-divorce I took my kids across the country, camping all the way. It took two months and it was the only time in my life, other than when I was a child, I felt completely free of men—their pull and complications. Sometimes I miss that early post-divorce period, but that's not what this is about.

There was another couple with us the day we went to Butchart Gar-dens. The woman was skinny with lanky hair, bracelets, a flowing cotton skirt. It's what I aspired to be though I was thickly set in hair and body, and self-conscious because of it, so I dressed boyish. I probably wore cut-offs and maybe a peasant blouse. They were popular then, with their elas-tic necklines and short sleeves, fake embroidery. Likely the other girl's blouse had real embroidery, and soft suede straps from her sandals wound around her delicate ankles. Somebody had a small power boat. We left from the beach at Brentwood Marina, a place where, in later years, my parents would moor a vintage wooden cruiser, and between cruises would drink beer and eat appetizers on the dock with the other boat owners who moored there. During that time my first husband and I would marry in the park skirting the Tsartlip Reserve, and years later my second husband and I would take our kayaks out on the blue waters and paddle a long way down the Saanich Inlet to a place where, to this day, a heavy set of stone stairs drops through the woods to the shore, rumoured to be the residuals of a movie set from sometime in the mid-twentieth century.

WJOŁEŁP, as it has been known for thousands of years in the SENĆOŦEN language, was renamed Brentwood Bay in 1925 after a town in England where the president of the BC Electric Company once lived. That day in the late seventies, the bow of our craft nosed along the surface of the bay parting the water before us, so we were certain, without saying, without even thinking, that the bay belonged to us.

Back then I knew nothing about the original inhabitants of the bay, nor did I know anything about flowers, though I was reading *Small is Beautiful* and *Diet for a Small Planet*, and knew something was very wrong with the world. Nevertheless, giggling and indifferent to world problems, we passed thick joints between us in the crowded open boat on our way up SṈITW̱EŁ, "the place of blue grouse," or what the settlers renamed Todd Inlet. We slipped by giant maples and graceful arbutus that lined the shore. Thick patches of salal camouflaged the moss-covered ruins of the old cement plant. But I wasn't thinking of history or language or a lost culture. I was high and silly, the sun was warm on my back and the boy's eyes were as blue as the sky. The weed loosened my tongue and believing everyone thought me clever, I chattered wittily. The boy, who sat behind me, shifted the motor first this way then the other. I sensed the tautness of his muscles, and the air was mixed with the smell of motor fuel and human sweat, the sweet and sickly fragrance of marijuana, the salty sea.

Somewhere we found a beach to land and the boy eased the boat to shore. We scrambled out and heaved it above the tide line, then picked our way up the bank through tangled blackberry, snowberry and wild rose. We emerged out of the forest into a sunken garden. Its sides were resplendent in variations of colour and density and shape, all of it, taken whole, blurring together like the image in a kaleidoscope. The air was heady with the scent of flowers.

Though I didn't know it at the time, the garden was on top of an old quarry from which the Butcharts extracted limestone to feed to their cement plants until they'd exhausted the supply. Limestone is a sedimentary rock layered with tiny fossils and shell fragments. In this way it contains the history of a place. With the limestone used up and the former quarry now beneath the careful arrangement and management of exotic flowers and shrubs, the history is concealed.

What has stayed with me from the day we snuck into Butchart Gardens isn't the boy, whose interest must have waned because I know I didn't see him again. I don't recall a kiss, even. Perhaps there wasn't one, or it was so unremarkable I've forgotten. What stayed with me is the thrill of invasion, the sense of triumph that we got away with a stolen entry, how our presence there added another layer of deception.

## iv) House of Floods

Cook Street, Victoria

Some years ago, around 1983, a realtor stood in the empty living room of a house on Cook Street in Victoria and told a young woman and her husband at the time that the house had *good bones*. The young woman said it was the same vintage as her childhood home on Herd Road. With a baby on her hip, she swung her free arm around pointing at the coved ceilings, worn oak floors, the gaping brick fireplace that she would learn stole all the house's warmth. Her blonde-haired, ponytailed husband stood beside her, grinning at her delight. She especially loved the glass-panelled French doors dividing the dining room and the living room, their only imperfection a tiny crack that meandered across one of the panes like a contour line on a map.

The house was on busy Cook Street two blocks from an even busier intersection at Quadra Street, one of Victoria's main thoroughfares. This wasn't the end of Cook that skirts Beacon Hill Park, where the houses are Edwardian. It was on the other end, where the woman saw a mouse run across the aisle at a grocery store in the neighbourhood. Cook Street was named after a British explorer and cartographer who, without ever inhabiting the land, mapped its coastlines.

The young couple moved into the house, and as the years went by the delight on the man's face faded, and sometimes bottles containing whiskey appeared in the dank corners of the basement, and the man would drink from them. Another child was born, and the house filled with the sounds of children, its worn floors sprouted bright plastic toys, and in the backyard a wading pool and a swing appeared. The woman refused to remove the English ivy that crept up the trunk of the massive oak, and in the shaded garden that bordered the fence she planted impatiens.

Several stately oaks lined Cook Street, a reminder that the city was built on a Garry oak woodland, a rapidly disappearing ecosystem overcome by development and invasive plants.

In the way that water shapes rock in a bay, the woman learned the house just as the house learned the woman. It absorbed the smells that she and her family brought to it, the walls echoing the sounds of their voices and movements. Its rooms took on their favourite colours, and each small dent and crack contained their stories. And in the way of rivers and mountains as well as shorelines, the placement of its walls, its passageways, its entrances and exits, imposed constraints. The view from the front room window was of a busy street. Sometimes during the day, the woman would pause in her tasks to watch the traffic pass by.

When her children were six and three years old, the woman came home from the hospital, where she'd been for several days with a cast on her leg and stitches in her head. A car had thrown her out of a crosswalk. After a few weeks of immobility, the doctors enclosed her ankle in a walking cast, and she was able to walk her children to school. On leave from her job, it was only she and the house throughout the day. She dragged the weight of the cast behind her from one room to the other, tidying, folding laundry and cooking, all the time fighting fatigue, vertigo and pain. The only sound was the scrape of the cast on the hardwood and the whoosh of traffic on the busy street outside. The walls, with their many tiny imperfections, began to close in on her, as if slowly pulling her body into the house's *good bones*. She had an urge to obliterate the walls with her casted foot and the help of a sledgehammer, but in the way her mother had taught her, she settled on whitewashing them instead. Her mother said white brightens a room. Standing on her one good leg and her other casted leg, she rolled the sopping paint roller over the bumpy surface, working while the children were in school and not sleeping after they were in bed, with the aches in her leg, hip and back. How the room would swirl, and she would rub the place where the stitches had been sewn into the flesh on her head. Within days, the living room and dining room shone with a satiny latex concealing the layers of paint beneath. The woman began to heal, and months later her husband moved out.

The years went by and the weeping tiles around the house deteriorated. In the winter, rainwater flowed down the driveway from the street to the basement door and eventually crept through the abandoned sewer outfall beneath the lawn, along the broken perimeter tiles, between the cracks in the foundation and into the basement. Storms drove the woman from bed in the middle of the night to mitigate the flood damage. When she stepped outside the door in her housecoat and rubber boots, the cold wet air shocked her awake. She scooped water from the backed-up drain until she scraped bottom, and the bucket came up empty. Afterwards, she'd pause for a moment, her sleeves wet and heavy at her wrists, and stare into the murk where the streetlights blurred the wet air. In the few hours before dawn the street was empty of traffic, silent except for the sound of the rain, and the rain became a lullaby.

A friend who read Tarot cards came for tea and spread the cards on the coffee table. The friend asked, "Have you figured out what you were doing in that crosswalk?"

"Walking in the lines," she said. She'd always thought that's what you were supposed to do. She began to realize that in her life there was something missing, perhaps herself, and it would take a lifetime to properly answer her friend's question.

With all the rain, mould crept up the insides of the walls, one floor at a time, and eventually the rats squeezed into the attic through the roof vents. The woman knew what the house needed, but she was also learning the limits of her own ability to provide. If she could have afforded to fix the drainage, she might have solved the problem once and for all, but all she could afford were exterminators, who had to come three times. Some problems are unsolvable or only partially solvable, so, like effluence, they have a way of becoming once again present in a life. Year after year, the basement flooded.

..

Victoria, being a port city with temperate weather, has always had a rat problem, and in recent years has consistently placed on British Columbia's "rattiest" list. Also, in a tourist destination, known for its double-decker buses and hanging flower baskets, its Empress Hotel with the tiger skin pinned to the wall in its famous bar, the existence of rats, were it better known, would be bad for business. In Victoria one didn't talk about rats. One barely talked about one's basement.

For forty-five years Captain James Cook's statue stood on a pedestal above Victoria's Inner Harbour facing the Empress Hotel. Then in 2021, long after the woman had moved from the city, the statue was toppled by a group protesting colonialism and its base was splattered with red paint in plain sight of the tourists. It was replaced by a makeshift statue of a red dress commemorating missing and murdered Indigenous women.

..

Sometimes her mother stayed with the children when the woman worked the night shift. While she was away at work and the children were asleep, the mother liked to get into the house's corners with the vacuum cleaner and buckets of soapy water. She removed spider webs and scrubbed away encrusted food. One morning the woman returned from work bleary-eyed as usual. The children were still in bed, but her mother, always an early riser, sat at the kitchen table with a coffee and a cigarette. The daughter hadn't slept for more than a few hours for days, and that restlessness that jangles the insomniac body crawled about her legs and made it impossible for her to sit, though she'd always enjoyed these early morning conversations with her mother. She began to clean the fridge, tossing items that hadn't even reached their expiry date, the house filling with the stink of bleach. The mother lit another cigarette and sat at the table watching her daughter. The young woman asked her mother to help move the fridge out so she could clean behind it.

The mother shook her head. "I did it last week." Then she rose to pour her daughter a cup of coffee and told her to sit down. The woman obeyed. She folded her arms on the table and dropped her head into them. Her mother placed a hand on her daughter's back and said, "Your life is just like mine."

..

There comes a time when you know you're done with a house, when it's done with you. The woman knew now she'd never repair the crack in the French doors, and the house would always be damp and cold. The children were teenagers now. The woman wanted a new house.

## v) House of Tea

Point Ellice House, Victoria

It's 2019, the summer before the pandemic. I'm in Victoria for a few days and am waiting for a friend in a restaurant on the gentrified Selkirk Waterfront, where the streets are nouveau brick, and where my second husband and I once briefly considered buying a luxury condo. Outside the massive floor-to-ceiling windows, dragon boats slip by on the Gorge Waterway, rowers in motion like so many pistons in a machine. It's a warm evening. Voices and laughter drift through the open doors from the pedestrians and loungers on the wooden boardwalk above the sea. Inside the restaurant, relaxed chatter, the clink of glass and cutlery, merge into a congenial buzz. And at intervals, the earsplitting sound of metal shattering metal from the nearby car-crushing plant. No one seems to notice—not a pause in conversation or glance toward the window.

A grove of trees across the tiny bay and beyond along the shore catches my eye. The blur of greenness softens the view of broken cars and piles of flattened metal. A memory arises: an old house where I once took my first mother-in-law, and schoolgirls in bonnets served us tea. Was it before or after my divorce from her son? My mother-in-law's parents were from England, and she'd taught me how to make shepherd's pie and the roast beef with Yorkshire pudding that she served for Sunday dinner on Royal Albert English Fine China. Several of my schoolteachers were recruited from England. Growing up in Victoria, I learned early in my life that the standard to which we aspired was English.

The old teahouse of my memory was a Victorian house, tucked away behind trees, a refuge amidst the clang of industry even then. We would have sipped from delicate teacups and nibbled on pastries while the rough world encroached from beyond. Today I sit in that rough world, though the waterfront has been gentrified, and the restaurant offers an extensive list of local beers and wines, a twenty-first-century refuge.

I'm curious about the grove of trees, the memory of tea. I open Google Maps on my phone. I get my bearings and look for something that might represent a teahouse. My eyes scan over blue balloons indicating a welding service, a steel company, a distillery and a landscape/gravel mart. And off to the side, toward the shore, there is a tiny street named Pleasant Street. I click on the balloon and the words *Point Ellice House Museum and Gardens* appear.

In this cartographic depiction the house exists only in name. It's not visible with the eye out the window behind the trees, though my memory now recalls its presence.

..

My first mother-in-law grew up above Westbay Marina, not far from where I sit in the restaurant with the grand windows. She lived in a Steamboat Gothic house featuring a tower. It was built in 1893 by a Captain Jacobson and several years later rented to my mother-in-law's family. The tower "oriented four-square to the compass" enabled the captain to keep his eye on his sealing ships at the marina below and the Victoria skyline beyond. He made his money as a sealer, thus contributing to the near decimation of the fur seal population off the northern Pacific Coast. From the vantage point of his tower, he stood at the axis of his universe.

But this had little to do with my mother-in-law, who was opposed to clubbing seals and had a whimsical romantic bent, so was well-suited to growing up in a house with a tower. I imagine her standing there as a girl shifting her gaze from one to the other of the four directions. Did she dream of England? Where she'd never been but from where, rumour had it, her father had fled for some minor offence, followed by her mother soon after.

..

My friend is a few minutes late, so I do a further Google search. Point Ellice House in its twenty-first-century version is a nineteenth-century home and garden open for tourists. There's no mention of a tea room. A photo of an interpretive plaque from 1969 describes its early owner, Peter O'Reilly, as magistrate, judge and gold commissioner, all prestigious titles in the colonial Victorian society of the time. I can't remember why I took my mother-in-law there. It was sometime in the early 1990s, and I believe it was only the two of us without husbands or her grandchildren. Was it after her husband died, and she was so often at what she called "loose ends"?

I enjoyed our conversations. She liked to tell stories about her family: a niece who was a leading artist in the Dada movement, and a brother she never forgave, not because he supported the Sandinistas, but because he left his boom box to them instead of her when he died. There were a couple of card-carrying members of the Communist Party. Her ilk was unconventional because, unlike my mother, with her carefully guarded family background, my mother-in-law felt no pressure to fit in, to disappear into conformity. She'd already effortlessly achieved a level of prestige: her home in Fairfield, the

English family background, her husband's employment at the Empress Hotel.

I was nineteen when I dated her son, my first husband. He took me to meet his parents, who still lived in his childhood home in one of Victoria's oldest neighbourhoods. In a nook off the entrance to the house sat a chaise lounge, next to a cabinet with glass doors containing books and Royal Doulton figurines on glass shelves. Now and then, we'd catch his mother scrubbing the kitchen or dusting to Wagner on the turntable at full volume, and she often parodied lines from *Carmen*: "Toreador, don't spit on the floor. Use the cuspidor." I wasn't familiar with such lighthearted irreverence, the humour in my family so often shadowed and mocking with a note of pain. She was fond of spoonerisms, frequently said "It's time to met a goove on," of puns and malapropisms, and she was fond of me.

She's been dead for years. When she was in hospice, my first mother-in-law said, "You didn't believe I had cancer."

"I didn't want to," I said. Then she told me she wanted me to get back together with her son. I knew it would never happen, so I said nothing.

If the outing to the Point Ellice House occurred after my separation from her son, we'd have carefully avoided any discussion around the break-up, the conflict, the emotions. We would have discussed arrangements my ex and I had made for when the children would see their dad, whether I'd continue to manage in the house. We'd have discussed the architecture of the tea house, the objects behind the glass doors of the built-in cabinets in the gracious former dining room.

During that outing, we wouldn't have known or have had the opportunity to learn about O'Reilly's other significant role in BC history. O'Reilly performed many functions for the colonial government of his time, but the role that had the most far-reaching impact went unmentioned at Point Ellice House until 2019, when the tea room closed and the house became a museum. I sit at the restaurant with the large windows on the gentrified Gorge Waterway and I read on my phone's tiny screen about O'Reilly's other role in the making of the colony. He acted as the Indian Commissioner between 1880 and 1898, during which time he single-handedly drew a Cartesian blade across First Nations territories, ultimately establishing over six hundred reserves in British Columbia. He did this brusquely, efficiently and with minimal input from those most effected by his decisions.

..

I never lived like a Victorian during my thirty years in Victoria, living the Victoriana dream, in a heritage home steps from Beacon Hill Park. Rather the park was where my brother, as a young gay man in the late seventies on the brink of the AIDS epidemic, looked for love after dark, while a friend and I did LSD and watched the limbs of the trees become human limbs. Where recently a homeless camp sprawled across the ordered landscape just beyond the tidy beds of flowers, and where First Nations' graves were discovered high on the hill. It's a weary relationship I've had with this, my hometown. I've despaired of its strangulated Englishness, the murdered teenage girl under the pretty Gorge Bridge, its eruptions of violence, all despite its flower-stuffed-basket-lined streets. History ekes through the fabric of this veneered city.

..

That time we had tea at the Point Ellice House, my mother-in-law wouldn't have known any more than I did about Peter O'Reilly's role in the relegation of Indigenous people to reserves. I don't recall a conversation with her about my First Nations heritage, though it seems to me she knew, as I wouldn't have felt there was any reason to conceal it from her. We had many conversations back then, on everything from children to socialism. She voted for Pierre Elliott Trudeau, likely supporting his desire to abolish the Indian Act and the reserve system under the guise of creating a *just* society through his White Paper. She wouldn't have seen how if it had passed it would have enshrined assimilation and rendered my Indigenous ancestry even more invisible. If I'd thought of it at the time, I suppose I wouldn't have seen it either, or thought it relevant. As for my mother, she wasn't interested in politics.

I have no memory of going to Point Ellice tea house with my mother. She would have enjoyed the fine china and the lace tablecloths, imagining herself as a Victorian lady. It's possible I simply prefer not to remember her at a Victorian tea house. When I think of my mother and tea, I think of the Royal Albert Old Country Roses cup from which she drank her morning coffee and occasionally tea, the very cup from which I now drink. Instead of her at a Victorian tea house, I like to think of her old friend Madame Brenda, the teacup reader, hunched at the dining room table over my mother's cup, drained of all but the remaining tea leaves. Her eyes are closed and she's murmuring in a throaty voice while my mother beside her is rapt and jotting notes.

..

I close the site on my phone and push it aside on the restaurant table. Maps are as reductive as the allocation of reserve lands, as reductive as the quantification of blood and lineage. And yet they have the power to claim.

I miss these two women, one for the life she gave me, the DNA, the struggle and the resilience, the other for her aplomb, her faith that no matter how much she strayed from the path, the world would keep her safe. They were both courageous.

..

My friend arrives at the restaurant, and we hug. It's been a while and there's much to talk about. Conversation drifts from her workday, its frustrations, my drive down island, the changes in the city, its building boom and the high cost of living, the homeless camp off the highway, and as the evening light falls, to us, our most recent disappointments, our dreams. The darkness presses on the outside windows, but inside it's well-lit. The babble, chiming of cutlery against dinnerware and bursts of laughter have faded to background noise. The roughness, the noise from the car-crushing plant, ceased for the night.

..

Point Ellice House officially closed April 22, 2023. The non-profit group who operated it couldn't find funding, and the house was falling to ruin. Much had changed in the world since I'd found the place on Google Maps almost four years before. These days, conversations turn quickly to climate disasters, the health care crisis, the city's ever-increasing numbers of unhoused, and sadly, only sometimes, to the ever more discoveries of unmarked graves at former sites of residential schools.

I happened to be in Victoria the day the house closed. The lineup stretched from the entrance gate along the flower beds brimming with daffodils to the house's front door. We were surrounded by the racket of shattering glass and the roar of backhoes from across Pleasant Street. They only let a few of us in at a time, but still the narrow hallways were thronged with people jostling to see beyond the roped-off rooms with their high ceilings and elegant furniture, lush Indian carpets, and Victorian bric-a-brac filling the narrow shelves.

At the entrance to the drawing room a bear skin sprawled across the floor, claws and head intact. Across the hall, where the bear seemed to direct its gaze, stood an interpretive panel titled *The Geography of Settler Colonialism*. Peter O'Reilly's office.

A quote on the panel read: "Having visited this reserve three times, I came to the conclusion that the extent of land claimed by them was out of all proportion to their requirements. (Peter O'Reilly, 1868)"

The room was spacious with two windows, one with a view out to the water. The furnishings exuded comfort. A bloated wooden desk took up much of the space in the way O'Reilly had in the colonial society that once held him in esteem. The wallpaper was faded and peeling in spots. The crowd had thinned. No one stopped to read the panel.

## vi) Childhood's Mountain

Mt. Prevost, Cowichan Valley

It's not surprising my brother wanted his ashes spread on the mountain, though he didn't tell anyone but me before he died in 2006 at the age of forty-eight. I don't remember the conversation—perhaps there wasn't one, and it was just one of those things that I knew. When I told my family, all but my mother, who said nothing, nodded in agreement. It made sense.

In the following years my mother cloistered his ashes, as if they were my brother himself, in the back of her closet surrounded by her silk scarves, her smell. She said she needed just a little more time. How we cling to the remnants of our dead.

Six years after his death she was finally ready to relinquish the ashes to the mountain. That's what we called Mt. Prevost—*the* mountain—using the definite article as if it belonged to only those who inhabited its base. More than our adventure playground, it backdropped the rural neighbourhood in which my family lived just outside of Duncan. With its forested slopes, stony ridge and dangers, it stood as an edifice to childhood. Our houses were located far below its peak on acreages that accommodated a few hens, a goose or two, and in a fenced field a Hereford steer for butchering in the fall, perhaps an apple or a cherry tree too. Our families were not serious farmers, but motivated only by a belief in the thrift that comes from growing one's own food and a desire to live on the outskirts. My brother named our steer *Danny*, and we fed it tufts of grass. We made up stories about Danny's life. After Danny was butchered none but my father would eat the meat despite being told Danny had been expensive.

We were country kids in the 1960s, when mothers shooed their offspring out the door in the morning on weekends and holidays and told them not to come back until dinner. Only my baby sister, when not dangling awkwardly from my arms and being hauled around the yard as a prop in our imaginary games, was permitted to stay in the house at my mother's side. My two brothers, myself and our pals moved as a coruscating unit across each other's properties and along the highway, where we motioned to the serpentine logging trucks to sound their horns. We slithered beneath barbed-wire fences, past curious cattle and beneath the power lines and through the third-growth forest to the summit of the mountain. We imagined cougars and Nazis, murderers of children in the woods. So much wildness and so much freedom from the constraints and rages of our working-class homes. I look back on it as a holy time.

On the day we would spread my brother's ashes, the plan was for my sister, myself and our husbands to hike to the mountain's summit—where we'd meet our parents, who would drive. We'd then say a few words about my brother and handful by handful toss his remains to the forest below. I'd hoped for a nostalgic ramble beneath the power lines, our childhood route up. I see now that what I'd hoped was to be flooded by memories, to recover some shred of my youth. But mostly, I imagined I might find my brother there.

The trailhead was far from the base of the power lines, and I began to doubt my memory. We wound upward on a path I didn't recognize and made a series of wrong turns. The woods were covered in a film of late summer dust and choked with blackberry. Nothing came back to me. It had been such a long time.

My sister, who was attempting to keep in touch with my parents by cellphone, lost contact. During the last half of the ascent, we fretted that they were driving in circles somewhere on the mountain's labyrinth of narrow gravel roads, or worse, that they'd been knocked into the ditch by a logging truck carrying a teetering load of logs.

Two hours after leaving our cars below, we reached the summit. The wind had picked up and the branches of alders rubbed alongside one another, making a high-pitched squeal like the sound of a cougar. The small parking area near the edge of the cliff was empty. We stood in silence, catching our breath, sipping water and sharing trail mix. The Cowichan Valley stretched out below, a patchwork of farmland. Not far from where we stood, atop a sheer cliff, a ten-metre cenotaph pointed like a finger to the sky. I'd forgotten about the war memorial, unchanged, a commemoration to fallen soldiers of the two world wars. It occurred to me that my brother's ashes would lie on a slope below it, as if it were him being honoured. I smiled at how he would have enjoyed the irony of that. He was no soldier, but hadn't he fought his own personal wars?

My sister tapped my parent's number on her phone. No answer. The wind lashed, and we stood there wordless. All we could do was wait. After a few minutes, they pulled into the parking lot and my sister whispered, "Thank God." My father bustled out of the car, laughing at the calamitous trip up: the confusing network of roads, the dodged logging truck, the dead cellphone. My mother remained in the passenger's seat staring straight ahead. I opened her door.

"Mom," I said.

"It's windy."

I shrugged. "Are you getting out?"

"I'll have a look."

"Okay, it's only a short walk," I said.

My mother hugged her cardigan to her chest and moved against the wind as if pushing it out of her path. She was a small woman whose silences were deafening. At the edge of the mountain's cliff she stood in silence, tightened her jaw and furrowed her brow. The tops of the trees corkscrewed in the gusts. It was a lonely place.

"Should we get the ashes from the car, Mom?" asked my sister.

Mom turned, and without looking at anyone, strode back toward the parking lot. "I didn't bring them," she hollered over her shoulder.

..

It would take another four years before my mother could release my brother's ashes and only on the condition we spread them on the beach near where I live. As she had in the past, my mother was tasking me with the job of keeping an eye on my younger brother. But now when I walk on the beach where his ashes were spread in the churning ocean, I cannot get a fix on him. It's only his absence I feel.

..

No one spoke that day on the drive down the mountain. I'd recently discovered that the mountain's name before the settlers changed it was Swuq'us, and it was once a sacred place for coming-of-age ceremonies. In the green blur that passed by outside the car windows, I imagined my brother, a child again, running with the ghosts of the young Quw'utsun.

## vii) Where the Loons Call

Fanny Bay

In the way the salmon return to the streams and rivers of their birth, months before my brother died, he came home to the West Coast after a lifetime away. Did my mother know the modular home with a distant view of the water halfway up the island would be her final home, in the way I wish this place of the loons north of Nanaimo and south of Courtenay to be mine? In her last hours did my mother think of Hope or Squamish, the mainland where she was born? Will I think of Duncan, of Victoria? Do we ever get to choose?

..

Loons are old souls. They are the oldest living birds, having an ancestry dating back thirty to fifty million years. Humans only date back about six million years. Loons, being much older than humans, are beautifully adapted to their water world—with their dense bones, "near the specific gravity of water," and a fine coat of waterproof feathers. How I wish humans were as well designed to meet the implacable nature of the world, had been as successful in ensuring our survival as a species. Loons spend their summers on the inland lakes where they have their babies. When the heat of summer mellows into the cooler days of fall, I look for them out on the ocean near my house, where they return to their familiar local bays and inlets.

..

You don't choose place any more you choose the family you're born into. Victoria, for me, held so much struggle, and on the pretty streets there was always the feeling that things were not as they seemed. But I grew up there. I learned to live with ghosts and what could have been. When I learned it, I could finally leave. I was compelled to move northward, where the coniferous trees hang heavy with seed in the spring, those millions of trees, what the logging companies name *timber*. I was drawn to those that survived beyond the shaved mountaintops, those on the radar of the developers. I'm interested in the ways of resilience.

Behind where I now live on the water's edge, between the old highway and the new faster highway, is a ravaged place of abandoned track and hidden shacks, a place used and left exposed by industry. And ten minutes down the old highway we walk the dog on the blackened beach at the coal hills in Union Bay. Here was where slurry from washing coal was dumped until 1960, and in its immediate vicinity the ocean is devoid of life.

..

I'm happiest here alone sitting on the shore near my house. It's early morning, and I'm scanning for a disappearing loon out on a silvery ocean. It dips beneath the water then reappears, and I follow it with my binoculars.

..

If I try to describe my mother, who is now dead, my self gets in the way. I'm not her and yet I have her DNA and only a few of her habits. We both moved from the city to the country when we were in our fifties, though I don't think she would ever have been content with all the sitting I do—at a window, in front of the computer, with a book on my lap. On their acreage in Mesachie Lake, a small community north of Victoria near Cowichan Lake, there was always so much to do—building a house and carving a garden out of the forest, for example. My mother was happiest with things to do. The lines between my mother and myself have blurred since she's died, and I'm trying to sort that out. What's me and what's her? My mother, like me, had she lived so close to the shore, would have been drawn to the beach at this hour to pick sea asparagus, pull out the invasive bindweed, sit on a log to listen to the loon's cry only long enough to have her first cigarette of the day. I, on the other hand, might wile away an hour on that log.

..

Personality is as elusive as this loon. There's a Buddhist meditation in which you imagine your body dissolving into light. If you do this correctly, which is more difficult than it sounds, you realize how impermanent the idea of a fixed you is, that so much of who you think you are is dependent on many factors, including time, place, the body, death, life. Who knows when the loon will surface again? I think of it warmly with its thick bones and ancient durable ways and imagine it diving for rockfish, flounder and herring, for sustenance, sometimes sixty metres deep. It's how I want to be in my last years. To dive deep, to say less, to listen more.

..

We're living in a time when people connect through social media and video-conferencing platforms. But more than half of communication is nonverbal and goes on in the quiet space between bodies. My mother's actual physical presence sparked and sizzled so that you felt as if you were beneath high wires. You felt a vibration from her. I miss her hugs, being close enough to bump up against the muscle in her compact body, the bone in her shoulder, a whiff of cigarette smoke and dish detergent. She was slow to trust and economical about her friendships, as she was in every other aspect of her life. I'm not saying she didn't have friends, because people were drawn to her, how her aloofness could suddenly flash into brilliance, into warmth.

..

Loons have several cries that warn of danger. The tremolo, most loved by human listeners, is made up of rapid modulations in pitch that tumble over one another. It's often referred to as the loon's "crazy laugh." They spend most of their time alone except during mating season when both parents raise the chicks. What I love about the loon is its elusive presence, unlike gulls whom I ignore for their ubiquity, their raucous indiscriminate congregations. Now a loon appears above the sea's surface, a soft blur in the distance, then just as I raise my binoculars to my eyes, it drops beneath the water only leaving a ripple. Another loon I can't spot through my binoculars emits a long low wail, a slight pitch in the middle of three notes, a vocalization that seems to travel across both distance and time. This is the *where are you, I am here* call. How it feels when someone dies. When I'm in anguish, I want to make a beautiful sound like the loon.

Now there are two loons. There's much flapping of wings and raising of breast, then some circling, then calmness as they swim parallel to one another, now and then dipping a beak into the sea. Though they drift close then move apart at least two metres, they never close that gap between them. Communication theory talks about the arc of distortion, how much can warp in the space between two points of contact. My mother and I never really understood each other. My interests were not hers. But when she was my age, she transformed a patch of alders and thistle into a garden. I take my family history and transform it into narrative.

..

How I wish I could sing a tremolo when I'm fearful of what's to come. I think of the raven who flew into my house one week to the day before my mother died. Such a dream-like event, though the raven left smudges on the front room window.

As the Spirits of the West Coast Art Gallery tells us in their writings on symbolism in Indigenous art, because "loons rely on water and water is a symbol for dreams and multiple levels of consciousness," it's best to pay attention to our dreams.

..

The loons are nowhere in sight and the tide is out. The beach is desolate. Loons are an indicator species, and they're threatened as we all are: by the acidification of lakes, climate change, encroachment on nesting areas, heavy metal contamination. It's late April and they're on the move to their breeding grounds. I wish I could go with them, while they wing through the air above the earth toward a sleepy warm lake, and when the time comes, rest on their backs like their babies do.

## viii) The Long View

### The Malahat

Near the summit of the Malahat on Vancouver Island the scenery opens to the meandering waters of the Saanich Inlet, its curved shores and humped, arbutus-adorned hills. I've driven this route hundreds of times in my life, and if it's not closed for snow, ice, floods or accidents, the highway is clogged with traffic, and someone is driving too fast, and my line of vision is sliced by strands of ceaseless rain from low-hung clouds. On those days, the windshield wipers slap in a flat note. I'm thinking only, as we do, of getting there. *There* for me is either Victoria on the island's southern tip, or north to Fanny Bay, my home halfway up the island. On rare occasions I've reached the summit and caught a glimpse of the inlet below shimmering in sunlight. On those days the sea, the land and the sky appear to meet seamlessly and float like a Shangri-La, a distant memory, and a feeling for ancestors enters me. I'm able to imagine grandmothers living generation after generation on the shores below. On those days, I am overcome by a visceral longing that I now know will never be satisfied.

From this location, I have an eagle's-eye view into the heart of the W̱SÁNEĆ people's traditional territory. At the centre of this geography across the inlet stands ȽÁU,WELṈEW̱, the sacred mountain of the W̱SÁNEĆ. Several times in my life, long before I knew its real name and I called it Mt. Newton, I hiked to ȽÁU,WELṈEW̱'s summit. From there, I looked across to the Malahat, whose name in SENĆOŦEN I don't know. Oh, that this strange language would unfurl from my tongue as if it had always been there, that I knew its words in my heart, but it's too late now.

A Buddhist teacher I once knew used to remind us that when you stand on a mountain you call it *this* mountain and the mountain you face is *that* mountain. But when you stand on *that* mountain it becomes *this* mountain. Something in this dizzying reversal of perspective reflects the truth of maps. So much depends on where you stand. Something in it also speaks to my relationship with Saanich.

A small ferry travels from Brentwood Bay to Mill Bay—from this shore to that shore—back and forth across the Saanich Inlet, enabling travellers to avoid the drive over the Malahat. Avoiding the Malahat is something most Vancouver Island residents like to talk about but rarely actually do because we like to avoid ferries even more, and the Malahat is the only highway that links the central and north island to Victoria. Sometimes all the conditions make it the inevitable choice—for example wanting to avoid rush hour traffic into Victoria when we need to cross the Malahat to head north, and the ferry schedule works—and we'll take the ferry from Brentwood Bay to Mill Bay. These conditions came together for me one summer day in 2021.

As the ferry departed the dock late in the afternoon, I climbed the metal stairwell to the benches above the car deck. I gulped the sweet salt-tinged breeze while my gaze wandered across the still water over to an area familiar to me, though it had been years. I scanned for the point of land that abutted the Tsartlip First Nation, where I'd married the first time, out on the rocks beneath the arbutus. I knew then I had relations on the reserve, but there'd been no contact for many years, so it was as if the wedding took place on the border of another country. The ferry ploughed the surface of the bay past Senanus Island, where I'd camped with my family when I was a child. Across the inlet the Malahat was rounded and blue in the late afternoon sunshine. It was a good day for a ferry ride. I welcomed the twenty-five-minute crossing and the hour-and-a-half drive home ahead of me once we landed at Mill Bay. There was much to think about.

Only an hour earlier I'd said goodbye to Brenda Bartleman from Tsartlip First Nation. We shared great-grandparents; her grandfather and my grandmother were siblings. We think this makes us second cousins though we may be removed at least once. Neither of us were entirely sure. She didn't remember my grandmother though I remembered her grandfather. My mother was fond of Uncle Bill and his wife Auntie Pearl, who had the same name as my grandmother. They came around to the house—he with his thick glasses and quick humour, she with her chit-chat and warmth. Didn't we go to their cabin on Gabriola Island?

"We probably played together there on the beach," I said to Brenda, wishing it to be so.

Over the previous months, I'd felt as if I was badgering Brenda with my emails listing questions about family and requests to meet with me, a stranger to her. She didn't recall my visit to her and her father in December 2000 with my mother. My mother and her father, who'd since died, would have been first cousins. During that visit Brenda told me that a family crest had been made on which wolves, which represent family, had been depicted. That was twenty-one years ago, and in the years since my interest in family history had waned until my mother died in 2015.

We've agreed to meet in a restaurant out on the peninsula near Brentwood Bay where Brenda, who's an Indian Registration Administrator for Tsartlip First Nation, often meets colleagues for meetings. On the drive out from Victoria where I'm staying with a friend, I manage to build a case against myself: *I'm an imposter... No, I only want to know something of that missing part of my history... Poser*, I tell myself, then *No, I'm doing this for my mother, I have a right to learn about my ancestry.* This all-too-familiar seesawing self-talk natters in my head the last few kilometres to the parking lot. I take a long slow breath then am able to enter the restaurant. Brenda hasn't yet arrived, so I settle into a booth and check my phone for messages. A few minutes later, the woman who walks toward me with a warm smile on her face puts me completely at ease.

Brenda and I are about the same age. We both have our grey hair pulled back in ponytails. I might be slightly taller than her, but neither of us are tall. We have much to talk about. She tells me about how my great-great-grandmother married a man from an area north of the Malahat, and when her father heard the man was mistreating her, he canoed there to bring his daughter home. It was after this happened that she married my great-great-grandfather.

"That's a beautiful story," I say. I'm feeling moved, brought close to tears by almost everything this near stranger says.

"It's not a story," she says. Her voice is kind but firm.

I recall her father, that visit to him with my mother in 2000—the strength in his voice when he'd told us about the ancient history of Brentwood Bay: W̱JOȽEȽP. How I could have listened to him all day despite not remembering the specifics of what he said. Now I wish I'd listened more. I know now he was a cherished elder.

"It's history," Brenda continues, this account of my W̱SÁNEĆ great-great-grandmother's marriage to my great-great-grandfather, Bartleman, a Scottish blacksmith. By this she asks that I not dismiss it as fiction, but regard it as worthy to take its place in the history that is now, not to be forgotten. Hers is an appeal to remember.

I share with her some of what I've discovered from my online research, and she nods; much she knows already. "We must get these histories down," she says more than once. She shows me a genealogical sketch listing some names I recognize from my childhood.

"You are of the ZIȻOT lineage," she says.

I'm silent, letting this knowledge settle on me, then I repeat the name of my great-great-grandmother until I get the pronunciation right. I feel the reverberations of that name in my chest as if I held an infant there. ZIȻOT, my great-great-grandmother, who once lived and breathed right on this land. If not for her, neither my grandmother, my mother, nor I would exist.

"Why couldn't I find this in my search," I ask, and immediately feel foolish.

"Oral knowledge, you wouldn't have."

Of course not. No one has ever told me about my great-great-grand-mother on my mother's side before. How estranged my family has been, how this living without history has left a void. There's something in Brenda's warmth, her practical nature—the sense I get that her load isn't light and yet she carries it with grace and strength, and perseveres despite doubt—that reminds me of my mother, maybe me. We hug and say our goodbyes, promise to keep in touch. But our separate complicated lives absorbed us once again, and it hasn't happened.

My car bumps off the ferry ramp and onto the road, and I've suc-cessfully avoided the Malahat. Traffic isn't bad. I drive north on the Island Highway toward home, away from Saanich. I pass through Duncan, where I lived as a child and where my auntie, Mom's sister, lives, a few hours' paddle from W̱SÁNEĆ. She's alone, so alone, but I don't have time to stop. I'll call her later. She'll want to know, and also not know, about my visit. She'll recall Brenda and that she both knows and doesn't know Brenda.

Though I've lived much of my life in the territory of the Saanich peo-ple, I've not known this land in the way Brenda, who lives and works amongst her people, does, nor as does W̱SÁNEĆ poet Philip Kevin Paul. In "Descent into Saanich," he's in an airplane above Saanich, and he knows "by heart" the sound the water makes on the shores below, and says, "The sound lays claim to me, a child of Saanich. *From under the tongue* some-one teaches me." The knowledge of where he comes from resides in his body in a way that it doesn't in mine. As much as I may try to claim it, this land doesn't claim me, three generations removed as I am. Standing atop the Malahat, I might as well be staring across the seas to Europe, toward my great-great-grandfather's Scottish homeland, a country I've never seen. I, who've camped uninvited on the local island Senanus, a sacred burial ground my family violated by our presence there, whose mother and grand-mother disavowed their mothers, am a stranger now. I will only ever know the land of the W̱SÁNEĆ people from afar.

# ROSE

Remembering

## Rose LeBlanc

April 3, 1937 – June 19, 2015

## ADVICE AS BREAD

### Comox Valley, 2020

Before my mother died five years ago, I told her she should live then I told her she should die. That's got to be akin to playing God. What audacity. Is this the sort of advice daughters should give their mothers?

It's best she was long gone before these COVID-19 days. She never had to live with a global pandemic, a marauding virus. My daughter quotes Facebook memes and maxims from health officials. We all do. Stay Apart to Stay Together. Stay Home. Who'd have thought it would have been so difficult? Humans are by nature on the move, dynamic, growing, changing organisms.

My daughter drops off homemade sourdough bread. Honeygrove Bakery is giving away sourdough starters. She's recently been extolling the virtues of fermented foods, how they enable thousands of busy little microbes to beneficially colonize our digestive systems.

The trick is to keep the starter alive. You have to feed it continually then add some to each batch of bread so that it's passed on from loaf to loaf like a genetic footprint. There's an interdependence between the loaves, the link in the sourdough culture.

So many people are baking that the grocery store shelves are empty of flour. And they're swarming the nurseries for seeds and little starter plants. At a time when the daily news tallies the worldwide deaths, people are obsessed with growth.

My mind imagines the virus shedding in an invisible vapour off the unknown infected, which could as easily be me or my neighbour. Wear a Mask. Stay Apart. Gratitude is urged. Be grateful. Be grateful again. Be grateful every waking hour of every COVID-addled day.

"Get outside," my daughter says. I take my sprout and organic tomato sandwich—keep yourself healthy—on sourdough bread out to the patio at lunchtime. They're putting in a new waterline along our road and the neighbours are building an addition. Loud large machines thud and rumble back and forth past my house, shatter the sound waves. "Sounds of spring," I say to my daughter and hold up the phone. "I moved to the country for this?"

"Assholes," she says. She enjoys swearing, like her mother, like her grandmother.

I tell her 113 people in BC died of an overdose in the opioid epidemic during March alone. By comparison, only 126 died from COVID-19 in two months. These are the early days.

"I know," she says.

Of course she knows. She's a social worker, as I once was. She hears facts every day that most of us would prefer to ignore or deny.

"Where's the money for that epidemic?" I ask, meaning the opioid crisis.

"Don't read the news so much."

*What news? You call that news?* I want to say, but don't because she hates it when I ask those kinds of questions, make those kinds of provocative statements, and she doesn't have a lot of time. And I don't want people to mistake me for a conspiracy theorist, an enemy of the state. My daughter doesn't need that. Besides, I know for sure I'm not an enemy of the state or a conspiracy theorist. Maybe a bit oppositional, but who isn't, especially these days, and my daughter's okay with that bit. And what is that anyway, oppositional—someone who opposes the status quo? My daughter and I are drawn to people who don't fit the mould.

..

Once my mother worked in a group home for adults with mental health issues. One of the residents was in the home because she had cut off her own arm at the elbow with an axe, and it was this woman, this one- armed woman who wrote poetry, that my mother bonded with. While the other residents watched TV, the one-armed woman and my mother took their cigarettes out on the porch with one of those old-fashioned monster amber-coloured ashtrays and talked and smoked their brains out. The woman told my mother all about how the voices ordered her to harm herself because she was a "piece of shit"—their words. My mother advised that broken, self-loathing, limb-severed woman to kick those assholes and jerks across the planet because what did they know. My mother knew beyond a doubt how good and special and entirely worthy of love that one-armed poetry-writing woman was, and she told her so every night for the two years she worked in that group home. And the woman would read her poetry to my mother, and together they would talk and fill up the ashtray until the night turned dark and cold and everyone went to bed and my mother's shift was over.

..

One time when I was six years old and walking home from school—I don't know where my older brother who usually walked home with me was that day—a boy in the grade ahead of me pushed me onto the ground. I can't remember why, only that I felt the pure injustice of that moment, and I went wailing home to my mother to tell her so. Her advice was to not take any crap from anyone, to march right over to that boy's house and let him know he wasn't getting away with it.

..

The year my daughter danced in a number from *Chicago* with her dance class, her boyfriend at the time insulted her, said something really insulting, and we'd both taken this boy for a gentleman, so charming. I wasn't there, but she told me afterwards that before she knew it her hand sprung out to smack him in the face. I could tell she was surprised by her reaction and feeling guilty. I'd taught my kids not to hit. I stared at her for a moment, then before I knew it I was singing "Cell Block Tango" from *Chicago*: "He had it coming. He only had himself to blame. If you'd have been there, if you'd have seen it..."

..

I take hostas and homemade chocolate chip cookies to her house. This, despite her earlier text: *Too. Many. Cookies.* She worries about sugar, but the twins have come to count on my cookies during this acetous time, and it means I get to see them. My mother always liked hostas and brought them to me when we moved into our new house a few years before she died. They're hardy, shy in the winter and brash in summer in their full foliage; they brighten the shade. Much like my mother, and my daughter, come to think of it.

My daughter stands in the doorway on her porch with the boys gathered around her knees. They're chattery, smiley, small and intense with their mother's huge blue eyes, identical in appearance, and unbearably vulnerable and full of beans, piss and vinegar, and gentle—and sweet as a chocolate chip cookie, for which they're now rifling through my bag. My daughter rolls her eyes and reaches for the pot of hostas, thanks me. We're practising physical distancing, so she doesn't invite me in. I must be at least ten metres away in the middle of her front lawn. We have to shout. I exaggerate, but she does prefer to err on the side of caution.

"Put them in a shady spot," I say, "lots of water to start."

"The cookies?" She raises one eyebrow, thinks she's funny. The boys laugh. They adore her, as do I.

I tell her I went for a walk with a neighbour this morning, but it was very safe because the neighbour insisted we walk on opposite sides of the road. All the big machinery working on our waterline lumbered between us, severing our conversation. After a flatbed truck carrying a grader passed, I scanned the road for my friend, who'd become a silhouetted shape off on the horizon line. "I'm considering taking a pair of binoculars with me next time, a megaphone."

My daughter rolls her eyes again. "Don't walk with friends, for now."

"A latte would make it all so much easier."

She tells me to stop at Milano Coffee on the way home. "You can't go inside, and you have to wait two metres apart at the window. And the lineups are long."

I frown, then catch an expression on her face that reminds me of myself looking at my mother when she would say, "All I want is a cigarette." A certain patient scrunching of the lips and slight tilt of the head.

I tell her grocery shopping is insane, the arrows taped to the floor so confusing. "One day someone's going to get really mad at me," I say. "I'll be going the wrong way up a one-way aisle. Story of my life."

"I hate that people lean away and look down if you pass them," she says.

"What are you doing passing them? Go the direction of the arrows."

"Get your groceries delivered," she says.

The boys ask me to tell them about the grader and the big truck again, and she says she has to get back to work. How's that possible with twin three-year-olds at home and advice to keep grandparents away? The world expects too much of mothers.

On my way home I listen to the provincial health officer on the radio. "Be kind, be calm, and be safe." I hit the off switch and flip a CD into the player. Lucinda Williams's raspy voice sings "Car Wheels on a Gravel Road."

I grow weary of positivity, but my daughter's bread is very good—the staff of life. She wants me to remain alive in the way I wanted my mother to remain alive.

..

One day my mother was in her garden on the edge of the forest hauling wheelbarrows full of soil, flinging them by the shovelful, ordering my father around, and the next she'd taken to her bed in a modular home park set aside for seniors. At least, it seemed that sudden, though likely I wasn't paying any attention. For the next couple of years, she ate only what was necessary to maintain a tremulous breath.

I guess I'd always assumed her death would be an immediate and dramatic reversal of life: a massive heart attack in the garden, a brief battle with a vicious cancer fought fiercely to the end. I never imagined a gradual retreat into a small room where, though she'd always piled the bed high with plump pillows and freshly pressed matching linens, until then she'd never spent more than a few necessary hours a night. There's no honour in failing lungs, a slow diminishment of breath—what they named chronic obstructive pulmonary disease (COPD).

..

A life is accumulation—a culmination of, in my mother's case, years of cigarettes, long hours on her feet slinging meat trays in grocery stores, late nights vacuuming and making lunches for four children and a husband. Living with my father: that had to have aged her. My younger brother's death at forty-eight. A family history denied.

The "pulmonary loop" means the heart and lungs must work together. She drove life hard; it drove her hard. The heart can only take so much.

"Relax, Mom," we all said. "Relax. Sit down. Look at all the pretty flowers you've grown, and the children you've grown to adulthood. That article about your garden shop in the local paper, your repeat customers. The tidy pathways you've carved in the shadow of the forest. Rest." My mother's garden was a refuge to all but her.

..

She was brown-skinned, angular, not tall, brown-eyed, with a thick mass of black hair that she kept short. Slim and muscular. Matching pants and tops, smooth skin. People, feeling it necessary to name, said Italian descent, Greek maybe. Possibly Cuban. Never Coast Salish. She rarely spoke of her mother, never her grandmothers on her mother's side. Never Coast Salish.

In "Citizen," speaking specifically of racism, poet Claudia Rankine talks about people who "achieve themselves to death trying to dodge the buildup of erasure." My mother was described as *driven*, never sat still. My siblings and I always said given half a chance, she could have run a multi-million-dollar corporation. What was she striving for? Could it have been the opposite of erasure—visibility, to be seen?

On one of her hospital visits—there were a number, pneumonia, atrial fibrillation—my mother lay in a narrow bed in the hallway of the emergency ward waiting for a nurse, a doctor, a cubicle with a curtain around it, maybe some privacy.

"What's the point?" Eyes heavenward, her facial expression a power surge in spite of the quiet voice, her tiny, emaciated body.

..

The breath, nearly weightless and invisible, is as dependent on a body as a body is dependent on it. Breath is something you never think about, something that is always there like a mother, until it's not.

..

My mother was a woman who gardened by lamplight, polished floors at midnight, who got into college with a grade eight education. I was used to her trying hard. All she had to do was try harder to breathe. That's all. All she had to do was breathe. My mother, who had moxie in excess, couldn't muster up enough to know "the point." How hard could it be? It's not like I said, *For Christ's sake don't you owe us, don't you owe us eking out of every breath a life, every breath you can grab.*

"You have a job to do" was all I said. The hallway stunk like urine, like cleaner. I stared, maybe glared at the back of her head. Eventually she turned and looked at me. She was so skinny the high cheekbones on my firm-fleshed mother protruded. Famished, she was famished in those last days, and had no appetite.

"What job?" she said. A bit of spit flew from between her parched lips.

"Showing your grandkids how to age well." I'd been thinking about elders and their roles. At that time, I didn't yet have grandchildren, but my daughter had hinted that I might need to start preparing. I also knew that my mother had a very big soft spot for grandchildren. My daughter remembers how she used to draw bathtubs full of bubbles for her when she stayed for the weekend, and swimming at the lake—my mother was a strong swimmer. Running through the sprinkler. Water, warm summers, and all the cookies they made together.

I believe I did what my daughter calls shaming—body shaming, mother shaming, lemme die I'm done here shaming. My own mother. You're not done yet; you have a job to do. I told myself at the time it was advice is all, advice she likely never took. Or maybe she did. My daughter told me that my mother called her up a few weeks after she got out of the hospital that one last time and said, "Why don't you come up sometime and we'll get into the wine."

..

If she were here now, in this time of COVID, I would tell her to watch her lungs; that's where it gets you. Like my daughter says to me, I'd say "Go outside." I'd add "with your cigarette if you must, and your oxygen tank, though not at the same time." I'd tell her to get out onto her porch, that perch in the mobile home park on which she watched the moon rise above the mainland mountains. The last porch of her life.

She'd call me to make sure I was scrubbing surfaces with bleach, and she'd quote the numbers from the public health officer. She'd want to make sure I was safe. "Keep Safe," people holler at you when they pass you on the road at a distance or peek through your fence, on the phone or at the end of their emails. Keep Safe, and what they mean is don't get sick. Don't die.

Her last visit to the hospital came after a fall in the night that left her barely conscious, and they moved her to palliative care. We hovered and waited: my father, my sister and brother, my auntie and uncle, my daughter who took time off work and came every day. Had my mother been aware enough or strong enough or whatever it takes, she would have told us all to get out, go away from her bedside and do something useful: work in the garden, clean a bathroom, get some groceries in. My sister and I called her Mama. The nurses whispered, "Any time now." My father said, "Soon she'll go to sleep," his euphemism for death. He repeated it, not really speaking to anyone in particular, with a tentativeness in his voice, as if he wasn't quite ready to face the horror of her absence.

One evening during that week, my daughter was on her way home driving north along the shore on Highway 19A from Nanaimo. She stopped and took a photo of the sunset over the ocean. It was a particularly fiery sunset. "Grandma" was all she wrote in the text accompanying the photo she sent me. The women in my family believe in signs. It's all we have left. No spiritual or cultural life to pass on. Only a vague feeling for synchronicity.

Toward the end of the week the palliative nurse took me aside. "She's hanging on for the family. They do this." This woman watched people die every day. "She needs permission," she said. Since when did my mother need permission for anything?

I was the oldest daughter, and stupidly loyal and sometimes obedient. I held her hand and leaned close to ensure she would hear. My father, who'd again forgotten his hearing aids, dozed in the armchair. My mother always threatened to get him a megaphone.

"Mama," I said, "we'll miss you, but it's time to go; you can go now."

The evening sun lashed its last rays through the hospital window. My father stood to close the curtain.

My mother's eyes popped open. "Don't miss me," she whispered, then closed them again. Her last piece of advice; she knew well the pain of something missing. And that night she died—my advice, for once, heeded.

..

I'm not going anywhere today, no grocery store, not to my daughter's house. Though I'd never admit this to her, I get tired some days and I don't wish to go out into the world, not this world. It's at times like these I get it. Isn't that the job of a daughter, to get it, but of course I don't really because you never really do.

How could someone so vital as my mother merely fade away? Going is easy enough. The pull of those who need you, urging one another to eat, to rest, to stay safe, again and again, breathing in the best way you can— isn't that the point?

# A BIRTHDAY PARTY

Today, April 3, 2020, would have been my mother's eighty-fourth birthday, but she's been gone for almost five years. Gone, we say, and what we mean is bereft of breath, and bodiless.

The body has a history with a beginning, a middle and an end. In this way it marks time and scaffolds a life. Eighty-four years ago, on this day, oxygen entered my mother's lungs, blood pumped through her veins, and she began to smell, hear and vocalize, along with numerous other functions peculiar to the body. Years passed and her womb grew other bodies, four of us in all, mine being second, chronologically.

Though she was small, her body was in perpetual motion whether she was hefting a vacuum cleaner or muscling a tree from one end of the garden to another. Her physicality rippled like the rapids in a river, trembled and tumbled as if headed for the sea. In her later years, her taut and ready limbs sagged, her lungs laboured through COPD and finally lost their capacity for breath. End of the body's story.

..

When breath leaves a body, does what we call the person cease to exist? My mother's face stares back at me in the photo above my desk. We're seated on a patio at a café on a lake, that summer we drove through the Okanagan on our way to my niece's wedding. She wears her large brim sun hat, and the sun warms my skin. I hear her speak my name, *Jude*. She's almost relaxed that day: the lake in the background, children's laughter on the beach, our idle conversation. Relaxation didn't come easy to her. The photo is one dimensional though my memory of my mother is not.

..

It's hard not to think of death in 2020, with the daily reports of those infected with and dead of COVID-19, the warning that it will get worse. Public Health orders urge us to stay home, businesses are closed, and the streets of large cities are emptied out. The newsfeeds are flooded with images of the afflicted, attached to breathing tubes in hospital beds.

..

Though there's more to my mother's story than the history of her body, it's body and breath I yearn for on birthdays when the forsythias and daffodils are in bloom. I imagine her inhaling the springtime air as she strides toward me through a field of yellow blossoms, her smile and voice, her slender fingers capped with perfect nails reaching for me.

..

The virus is depicted as a space ball with spikes, its image all over the internet, now imprinted in our minds, yet there's no visual, auditory, olfactory, tactile or gustatory evidence of its existence. Well, unless you peer through a high-powered electron microscope and you know what you're looking for. If you were to analyze my DNA through that same microscope, you would find evidence of my mother. The virus was created by the exchange of genetic material, as I was from my parents. In this way, COVID is as invisible and at the same time as present as my mother.

..

It's been weeks since I've seen my father, though he lives only an hour away. He's shrunk to a tiny image on my iPhone, and his voice is faint, his face grey. Various inhalers are lined up on the table beside where his elbow rests. He doesn't remember it's my mother's birthday, or maybe he does, but he makes no mention of it, and nor do I.

The night she died my father called to say "She's gone," as if she'd stepped out for a smoke and hadn't returned to the building. I drove madly in the dark after midnight to the hospital, eyes bleary with fatigue and tears. Funny I remember it that way. Actually, my husband drove, and I was a passenger—aren't we all, and yet we think of ourselves as the drivers. We think we have a destination, though we never arrive where we believed we were headed.

..

I hold her photograph in my hand and update her on the latest, as if writing a newsy letter:

*You've got two great-grandchildren now, lovely boys, twins. Dad's moved into a seniors residence. It's good or he'd starve to death. You spoiled him with all you did for him, but you know that. His walls are covered in photos of you, and he has a sort-of girlfriend. Nice, but she's got nothing on you. Oh, and there's this virus.*

..

My mother and I will have a party today. I'll pick daffodils from my garden because there'll be no driving to town to buy a birthday present. The stores are all closed. Everyone's been told to go home. The provincial health officer started out by calling it social distancing, but now they're calling it physical distancing so people will better understand that it has to do with body proximity. Since her death five years ago, my mother and I have been physical distancing.

At five o'clock, I'll open a beer and listen to Hank Williams sing "Hey Good Lookin'," a favourite of hers. I'll dance around the living room the way she sometimes did with my father. I'll recall the swiftness of their vigorous limbs as they twirled and gyrated across the room, the small rush of air when they passed.

Sometimes my father leaves the seniors residence and drives his car up and down the nearly empty streets of Nanaimo looking for a shop, a restaurant with an open sign on the door. Before the virus, he would meet his sort-of girlfriend at McDonald's for a coffee. $1.29. He tells me it's a deal. The management at the seniors residence can't stop him from going out, but they have warned him of the risks. Visitors have been banned for three weeks, and now gloved and gowned healthcare workers—booties and masks are optional—deliver meals to his room.

..

No one knows for sure where my mother was born, and my father can't find her birth certificate. He used to tease her about being born in Spuzzum, a little spitball of a place in the Fraser Canyon. It was a myth that became a family joke, my mother born in Spuzzum with the nickname "Beyond Hope" because it was just north of a town called Hope, where my mother had lived during most of her childhood. She once told me she was born on Lulu Island, which is now the site of Richmond, a city in Metro Vancouver. This story seems the most plausible, though my father suspected my mother was making it up because she liked the phonetics of the words, *Lulu Island*, how spoken out loud, they pucker the lips and stutter like a soft Hawaiian surf, how the island was named after a child actress named Lulu Sweet and my mother would have liked to be connected to a pretty actress with a name like that. There's a birth story here lost to my mother and to her daughters, a missed history. A mystery.

After we kids left home, my parents moved to Mesachie Lake and my mother grew things on the edge of the rainforest beneath the clear cuts: forsythia, wisteria, hydrangea, dahlias, fuchsias. She believed that gardens, like children, were an expression of hope, a belief in the future.

Though she was named Rose, she didn't like roses due to their temperamental nature, nor did she like messy bold flowers.

..

In New York City they're talking about burying the bodies in Central Park, ten caskets to a trench because there are so many of them. In the past three weeks, 3,500 people have died from the virus in that city alone. There's always the problem of what to do with the body.

..

My mother was a great believer in discarding things that were no longer of use, annually and biannually clearing out drawers and closets, carting off bags full of clothes and household items to wherever she might be rid of them. It's possible she regarded the body in the same unceremonious way because when she died, no one in the family was clear on what her wishes were for its disposal. My auntie insists she wanted her ashes spread on the ocean so that she could "finally be free." Though my sister and I vaguely recall a conversation with her to this effect, my father swears she said nothing, had no plans, didn't want to think about it. In the end, he bought a plot and buried her ashes there, where his will join hers one day. Auntie refuses to visit the gravesite.

..

I confuse the numbers dead with confirmed cases, so many numbers each day, as if the lives they represent could be quantified, shrunk to a binary: dead or alive.

..

My mother is safe from the virus. From this, she will not die. Despite not having a body she manages to dance with me, sings along with Hank and tells me not to worry. Her voice is as I remember it, and she calls me Honey the way she did when I was a child. I mimic her body, how it twirls and dips, stomps and flows, breathless. Hank sings about the light, how he saw it, and I want to believe for my mother that there is no more sorrow in sight.

# BENEATH THE DIN

We were a noisy family, a lot of talking and thumping around. We hollered from room to room. My older brother, my younger brother, me and my baby sister, with the help of a dozen neighbourhood kids, doled out a particular brand of dissonance: shouting, scrapping, laughing, teasing, complaining. With her voice my mother fetched us from up the stairs, down the stairs, and off the porch, to dinner, to finish our chores, to go to bed, to school, to clean up our goddamn mess.

Her voice like a bugle at dusk summoning across the highway and the neighbourhood's backyards, over the fields and creeks, crepitating with exasperation. Sometimes she would sing in deep undertones. She liked the Hanks: Snow and Williams. Over a beer, she and her sister sang "Your Cheating Heart" complete with twang. My father told her she couldn't carry a tune in a bucket. Other than the Hanks and hushed parcels of neighbourhood gossip, for the most part my mother's voice was employed in the minutiae of household management.

On the other hand, my father couldn't abide the atmosphere in a room without the fullness of his sonance, the pandemonium of his opinions and the babel of his world view. As if to face off silence itself he spoke loudly of boisterous, misbehaving people: men who told the boss off, used their fists and took lovers, women who drank and danced in bunkhouse revelry. My father was a logger who worked with clangorous machinery in the dark, still forest. Even his body thwacked with judgement: footfall and thrown object.

..

I didn't speak at school in grade one, never raised my hand, said nothing in the schoolyard. My behaviour has since then earned a diagnosis in the *DSM*: selective mutism. At the time my parents and the teacher called it shyness.

During that year in grade one, I spent my recesses stepping gingerly over a border of roundish river rocks that enclosed a narrow garden along the front of the school. Back and forth I walked with arms stretched out at my sides, mind focused on maintaining balance. Back and forth, sometimes fast, sometimes slow, I practised daily. Winter came early in Prince George, where we lived for six years. It covered the schoolyard in snow, and the rock border was sometimes icy. I wore little red boots with a strap at the top and lining inside. My concentration grew stronger. Sometimes I slipped. The commotion of the schoolyard roiled around me, but for me there was only one red boot after another. I understand now that each careful step was a meditation, and its repetition a chant voiced by the body. It was a gesture toward equilibrium, which years later I sought in early morning meditation on my cushion, and my mother sought in her garden.

..

Soundlessness unfolds from the earth beneath the forest canopy. Or when the wind drops over the sea just before the tide begins to rise. Or when you face your reflection in a mirror, in a pond, in another's face. You can hear it. In my family, we pivoted around that kind of silence as if it were a hole we didn't want to fall into. If you didn't speak, you didn't exist. You became invisible. But sometimes it was how you wanted to be.

..

In July 2001, when Mom was still spending ten hours a day in her garden on the acreage my parents bought up island, she had to have a throat biopsy. Mom was a faithful smoker despite the COPD that would take her several years later, a chicken soup of lung conditions from too many cigarettes.

Sitting in my Victoria townhouse a few days after the procedure, I wrote in my journal:

*My mother gets up at six to go into the garden, and I get up at the same time to sit on a cushion and go into my mind. We're both in search of silence. She bending to the soil and me to consciousness, both of us losing our selves.*

My mother and I knew the weight of the self, how it was a trap, a demanding, fretful, cloying narcissistic clatter in the head from which we found respite in our own ways. She found it in the morning air on her skin, the sun that rose over the mountain, the smell of the dark earth and her strong limbs, the flow of blood to the heart: the stepping forward of the senses.

..

Despite a stutter my brother, who was only eighteen months older than me, was a great talker at home and at school. His rapid, fractured speech ratcheted above the voices of the other children, toneless, hysterical and trembling with colour. As if it had escaped from a region all but him knew to keep down. To be heard at home, it was necessary to wedge words in between his, and this skill served me in alleviating the loneliness I began to feel at school. In my nervousness, I interrupted conversations, talked between two talkers. Though I wouldn't have been able to articulate it, I'd learned by grade two that fitting in had a lot to do with saying the expected thing, or if you weren't sure what that was, saying nothing at all. I made friends and learned to fill silences. Sometimes, in doing so, I felt that I was becoming one of a loquacious mass that never really listened to one another.

..

The day after her biopsy, I phoned once I knew my father was up and would answer.

"Have you heard the results?" I asked.

"No, but she's fine."

"Is she talking yet?"

"No, but there's no reason she shouldn't be."

My father believed illness was something that happened in your head, like noise. He once removed a cast from his leg with a hacksaw.

..

In my journal I wondered whether my mother might, like the woman in Allende's *The House of the Spirits*, choose to live with but not speak to her husband for the rest of her life. She'd only communicate with him through her daughters, their exchanges brief and efficient. I wouldn't have blamed her, and for her, I would have willingly participated in such an arrangement. In her interactions with my father there would no longer be the need to choose between defending herself or submitting to his will, the crux of most of their exchanges. Would this have disarmed him, he whose words were a flint looking to ignite? Would this have given her some sweet quiet?

..

In grade eight, when we moved to Victoria, I again stopped talking. A kind girl whose father owned the corner store walked with me to school every day. "Why don't you say anything?" she asked. This did nothing to break the logjam of my speechlessness. I had no words, not a scrap of language, in my head. Only shame for the discomfort I caused. This went on for the rest of grade eight. I was grateful, and I'm sure she was too, when friends of hers joined us. Then I could relax, my silence dropping into white noise.

In this new neighbourhood, I had to learn the rules of social engagement, those that applied in a working-class suburban high school. The bad kids smoked pot on the fire escape and got expelled. The good ones drank jungle juice stolen from their fathers' liquor cabinets on the weekends. Pretty much everyone smoked their older brother's pot in the park. I discovered many ways to loosen the tongue.

..

After the surgery my mother spoke again. There was no cancer. She again found solace in the garden. I often wondered what came to her in the quiet hours spent there: a childhood rarely spoken of, inarticulate memory, the shadows of her Coast Salish grandmothers. Women unheard above the din, their silence a verb, an aggressive act.

..

Not long ago, I had a dream in which I stood at the mirror and noticed for the first time that my tongue was folded back into my mouth, so all that was in view was a half a tongue, looking like a spongy mushroom. How could I have missed this happening? Fearful that the two halves of my tongue had grown together from years of disuse and that I'd have to pry them apart, I reached cautiously into my mouth. With a slight touch, my tongue unfolded easily as if there were a tiny hinge on the crease at the fold. I woke relieved with an awareness that I had become the agent of my own choice to speak or not to speak, and also with a feeling of urgency that there was something, though *what* I didn't know, that had to be said.

..

I've participated in a couple of silent retreats in which I felt as if I was starting to get to the bottom of things, that feeling you get when beneath the water's surface, you swim free of the wave's disturbance. I discovered that everyday speech is at best functional, and at worst intrusive. Even a writer knows that words are only an approximation, and that truth resides in the inflections of the white space.

..

If you look it up in the dictionary, you'll see that silence involves a negation: noiselessness, soundlessness, speechlessness. An absence, but anyone who's experienced grief knows that absence has a presence in the same way that silence has an audibility.

# Shopping with Rose

In a black and white photo of my father and mother they're frozen mid-stride on a Vancouver sidewalk, circa late 1950s. It was taken by Foncie Pulice, the now famous street photographer. My older brother is absent, and I must have been in my mother's womb. Tiny pearls dangle from her ears and offset thick black hair cropped stylishly short. A jacket and skirt hug the contours of her shapely muscular body, and her feet are tucked into black patent leather heels. Her smile is wide, dark eyes sparkling, and her hand is in my father's. He wears a dandyish loose-fitting suit. He too smiles; it's maybe the only photo I have in which they look truly happy together.

I have a clear memory of my mother diving off the swim grid of my father's boat in a white bikini—she adored the colour white—her brown body slicing through the green water, disappearing then rising again seconds later in an eruption of sun-sparkled spray. To tell my father and her children how wonderful it was. And my father watching, laughing, beaming as if at a rare silver-skinned creature from the deep sea.

"She and her sister, so beautiful," said a cousin from my father's side at a family reunion a couple of years after my mother's death. I had a vague recollection of this cousin's once-flaxen hair, a shimmering, blue-eyed presence, but in that moment she stunk of cigarette smoke, and her hair was thin and limp. "It's that mix, don't you think, Dutch blood and Native blood?" she said, her voice dropping to a near whisper. She couldn't see past the hue of my mother's skin.

I don't recall the first time I saw my mother swim, though I know I was very young. In my memory she slides through the water, face down, neck twitching this way then that, moving away from the shore into the deeper parts. She told stories of a childhood swimming in the Fraser River near the town of Hope with her brother, how they had to avoid the whirlpools that would pull you down. Those whirlpools with their swirling, vicious water haunted my imagination. I couldn't help but think that the river might have taken her, my brave mother, and it wasn't that I feared I would then never have existed, because I was too young to understand how I came to exist, only that I had this crippling fear that my mother may not have existed. Time is neither linear nor logical when you're a child. There is you and your mother and mostly your mother, who you depend on, and because of that dependency love with devotion. She would assure me that her older brother was with her there in the river, and he kept her safe. I didn't yet know what unsafe was, I didn't understand the danger of whirlpools, only the warnings against rapids and water's depth. And I understood the coldness of river water because that's where I learned to swim too.

A few years after the street photo was taken, my mother dressed me in stiff crinolines and flouncy dresses as if I were her doll. I don't ever remember enjoying this primping. I was far happier in cut-off jeans and canvas runners shooting marbles in the potholed driveway with my brothers. I recall her pulling the brush through my thick hair, not pulling but yanking and twisting it into ringlets, her stern face in the mirror, my eyes stinging. Her disappointment.

I love the water, as all my family does, but I don't have her courage, the strength to shoot like a geyser above the water's surface. I think too much of what could go wrong, the ocean being a lot like my mother. How a storm can rise in a minute, how she could turn from warmth so quickly, how her tongue could lash. How she called me Honey in one breath and in the next told me I should stop eating potatoes because they were making me fat. Once, a few years before she died, when I complained about hot flashes, she said she had no time for menopause. This is how she survived. When my first marriage broke up, she said, "What should be and what is are often different." There was no talk of heartbreak, no gnashing of teeth, only a life to get through.

When I was about fourteen years old, my mother took me shopping for a bathing suit one day. I don't remember the trip itself, only the aftermath. No doubt I was surly and uncooperative, likely refused to try on anything, certainly anything she chose. My mother wanted me to be a bubbly, shapely, fair-skinned girl, a girl whose name ended in an "e" sound like so many of us born in the 1950s. But always I felt heavy, certain I needed to cover as much of my body as possible. I could never be as stunning as she was in a bathing suit, and it would have been a betrayal to even try. This truth, on some level, we both understood. What I didn't understand until I was much older is that what she wanted, maybe what every mother wants for their daughter, whether they admit it or not, was for me to know the leverage my body carried. She knew her own slender brown limbs had the power to beguile, the allure of exoticism. She believed it was all she had. My mother's looks made her visible in a world in which she would have otherwise gone unseen.

I remember clearly that we came home empty-handed after several agonizing hours together, and my mother, cold and silent, crashed around the kitchen while I retreated to my bedroom. When my father got home from work, I heard them murmuring about me, and moments later he pushed through my bedroom door without knocking, stinking of diesel from work.

"Nothing good enough for you?" He slid open my closet, reached in with his big working-man's hand, gathered up my clothes and thrust them all into a pile on the floor. "You don't know how lucky you are." I've never pretended to understand their marriage, his need to be her saviour when he wasn't being her monster, hers to have me in his disfavour. The image of a limp heap of garments tangled with wire hangers collapsed on my bedroom floor dominates my memory of that day.

..

It was the early seventies, one of those days after school midweek when my younger brother and I had been fighting over the stereo again—his David Bowie, my Joni Mitchell—while my older brother rotted in the basement surrounded by encrusted cereal bowls and blasting late afternoon TV. In the kitchen breakfast dishes were scattered across the counter, a pot with sticky porridge in the sink, and my mother's oldest girl child, embroiled in a sibling battle, neglected her chores. Mom would have arrived home from work to Bowie's thumping guitar.

At the sound of the car in the drive my younger brother escaped out the back door to join friends in some other basement, and I was in my room by the time my mother dropped the grocery bags on the kitchen counter. I flipped open the pages of *Adventures in English Literature* to my home-work, and in reading the line "Our birth is but a sleep and a forgetting" it was as if my soul rose above our 1970s working-class suburb and I knew for certain that I'd been displaced in time, born to the wrong family, and was meant for a higher existence. The music dead-ended outside my bed-room door, the laugh track from the TV rattled up the stairs from the rec room, water rushed from the kitchen tap, dishes clanked.

My mother's hard steps came down the hall, and there was an equally hard bang on my bedroom door. I didn't move until I knew she'd returned to the kitchen.

My mother didn't so much move through space with her wiry body and strong step as she parted the space before her as if it had a substance and a weight. And she made objects speak: the drag and crack of an ironing board, an iron bumped across shirt and pillowslip, a sofa raised to get at dust then dropped back into position, the squeak of cloth and cleaner on glass, rattle of dish and pot, pounding of bread dough on kitchen counter, hum of sewing machine. She could be a shouter and a foot stamper, though by the time we were teenagers she'd stopped chasing my brothers and me around the house with a wooden spoon. For such a small woman her steps were audible, and for someone who wasn't a big talker, she made a lot of noise.

I crept to the kitchen doorway and watched her brush her hand along the crumb-speckled counter to sweep a pile of cutlery clattering into the sink.

Now, many years later, looking back on this scene, I understand that she was weary to the bone, had put up with lewd jokes from that fat, pim-ple-faced butcher all afternoon, knew she stunk like sweat and red meat. Her youngest son had been skipping school and her husband blamed her.

Then there was me, her oldest daughter, who wouldn't wear makeup or cut the thick bushy hair that made her eyes disappear, those pretty eyes she got from her mother. And my mother knew that I looked down on her the same way my father did because I'd already gone further in school than she ever had, and because I got good marks, which impressed my father, and I was there, and my father wasn't. And because my mother knew full well her sons were as unconcerned with the ways in which they burdened her as was their father. Because my skin was white and freckled like his and hers was brown.

She couldn't help it. Some noise in her head that needed quieting made her reach under the sink, haul out the sopping garbage in its sopping brown bag and heave it across the kitchen. Plop. Potato peelings smeared with coffee grounds landed near my feet. I didn't flinch.

"This house is a pigsty," she spit out between tight lips. My mother used that expression often. These days, so do I.

"Now it is," I said.

What my mother saw was a teenage girl who, in that moment, she wished didn't belong to her. "Bitch," she said, her tone as cocksure as mine had been.

..

When I married the first time at age twenty-one, I wore a royal blue Indian cotton dress, and a crown of daisies circled my head; my flower-child phase. I'd found the dress in a funky shop that also sold incense and hookahs on Eighty-second Avenue in Edmonton, where my soon-to-be husband and I lived at the time. A few days before the wedding we flew out to Victoria, our hometown, and stayed with my parents. The ceremony was to take place in a park on Brentwood Bay twenty minutes from Victoria, where fleshy arbutus trees stretched their limbs above the ocean. We'd hired a Unitarian minister, and a harpist who played "Greensleeves" as I descended the wildflower-studded path to the point above the bay.

The park was adjacent to the Tsartlip First Nation, my mother's estranged ancestral home on her mother's side. We'd not, however, chosen the location for that reason. I remembered with fondness the two or three summers we'd camped on Senanus Island in Brentwood Bay when I was a child. My father sold the small boat that had taken us there, then bought a twenty-eight-foot cabin cruiser, after we moved to Victoria. The year before I left home at seventeen, and the two or three years after that, I'd spent some time with my parents on the waters of Brentwood Bay and at the marina, where powerboats lining the slips, much like my father's, bumped the wharves and left diesel trails on the water.

Despite our love of weddings, ritual, tradition and familial loyalty were thin concepts in my family. My parents never celebrated their wedding anniversary, and a few years before she died, I teased my mother: "Maybe you were never actually married." She'd tightened her lips and changed the subject. When I visited a few weeks later, my parents' marriage certificate lay on the dining room table. She'd found it in the back of her closet. She told me it had only been a brief civil ceremony, then she tapped the certificate to point me to the proof of their marriage. I realized then that I had hurt her. A few years later, hours before she died, she asked the hospice nurse for *the dress*, for the *white dress* she'd never owned.

The day before the wedding, my mother called me from work to ask that I meet her for lunch. At noon I met her in the meat department at Woodward's, where she slipped her apron over her head and threw on her coat, stepped out from behind the glass case she'd just filled with marbled cuts of meat. She had half an hour, we'd go into the mall and grab a hot dog. But on our way out of the store she steered me into ladies' wear. It was spring, late 1970s, and the clothing carousels were stuffed with a riot of pastel, neon and brightly flowered high school graduation gowns.

"Let's just have a quick peek," she said without looking at me. She thrust her hand into the dresses and flicked them rapidly along the rack, stopped at a flouncy fake silk off-white mid-length. "This is cute, not so formal. It could work."

"Mom, Mom." I leaned toward her. "What for?"

She sighed and fixed her wide startled eyes on me. "You can't... It's up to you, but it won't look right. Not blue for your wedding. What about the pictures? Your dad, he wants... he's taking the pictures... Try it on."

I stepped back and shook my head. "No," I said. I crossed my arms. It was not the first time I defied her, nor would it be the last. But it was the first time I said no, while understanding how it hurt—not just her, but me as well.

She bit her top lip and shoved the dress back into the pastiche of sickly colours, walked silently away from me.

..

I'm seated next to my mother at our kitchen table after dinner, cigarette burning in the ashtray at her elbow as she files off each ragged edge to shape her nails into perfect points. I'm still living at home with my parents, though I'm uncertain about my age at the time or how often this happens. I only know that I'm her appreciative audience, my ear attuned to the soft scraping of metal against nail, my mother's voice, her advice on how to use tiny scissors, pumice stone and hard polish. Her fingers that spend their days in animal gristle and astringent wash water are as slender as those of a pianist. Once she came at me with those nails, across the supper table. I don't remember what triggered it, only the scratch on my face afterwards.

"Your feet, too," my mother would say. "They're your foundation.

Take care of them." Footbaths, lotions and good shoes were not a luxury but as necessary as vegetables.

Not once in her life, not even in those last bedridden months, did I cradle her feet or her hands in my own hands and offer to paint her nails. I assumed that level of intimacy would have been alarming to us, but now I wonder if it was yet another way in which I rejected her, felt myself to be above her vanities—or even if that was untrue, that she saw it that way. Sometimes it was hard to know which of us needed the other's approval more. Love didn't flow easily between us.

..

The last shopping trip I went on with my mother also involved a wedding, my son's this time. Mom had come into a small sum of money when her oldest brother died. As a child, Uncle Lloyd had been placed in the Provincial Hospital for the Insane, whose name later changed to Woodlands School, in New Westminster. It was because he had a club foot and was said to be what we called "retarded" at the time, though I'm guessing it was institutional life that made him the way he was. Mom was the only family member who brought him home on holidays and visited him at the school, then at the shelter and, finally, in the care home. I remember him twisting and heaving his small body around the house in his big orthopaedic boots, his slow deliberate way of speaking. I recall his dark, pained eyes and wide, imp-like smile. He played the harmonica, and Mom hated how he cried when she took him back. He left her what remained of the money he made shining shoes in the shelter where he worked. She said he always liked me and would be happy if she used some of the money to buy me a mother-of-the-groom dress.

When I picked her up at their modular home in the seniors park in Nanaimo, Dad said it was the first time she'd been out of bed in two days. She bustled around the kitchen full of purpose. She'd touched up her face with powder and made her eyelashes as black and full as her hair, which she'd had professionally coloured every few weeks since it turned grey in her thirties. Her slight body crackled with energy that morning.

"I've called the store," she said. "I like to let them know I'm coming in, and they put a few things aside for me."

I'd been hearing about KC's Boutique & Petites for the two or three years in which Mom had become a regular customer.

"They carry Joseph Ribkoff. A classy place, and I always get the special treatment," she'd say, waving her palms. She was excited about taking me there, maybe about finally making it right, all those failed shopping trips with her oldest daughter.

We parked in front of Katy's at a strip mall next to Thrifty Foods, not far from my parents' house.

"We'll look for Susan. She's the best, and she knows me," said Mom. We were surrounded by racks stuffed with women's clothing, amongst which a blonde woman spoke with a customer. Mom guided me toward the dresses, all the time trying to catch the woman's eye. Finally Susan glanced our way, and Mom greeted her with a childlike smile. When she finished with the other customer, Mom introduced me. "She's a professor, you know, the oldest daughter I told you about. A professor."

Susan, cool and large-boned, not so much pretty as handsome, knew how to dress to make herself look lithe as a willow. To my relief, Mom's pronouncement about my profession didn't register with her, so it wasn't necessary to explain that I was, in fact, a part-time sessional at a hole-in-the-wall community college. Susan was unable to find the clothes Mom had called to have put aside, offered no apology and glanced frequently toward the door as the store filled up. After hustling me into the change room, Mom insisted the two of them huddle in consultation within earshot. I pulled off my clothes and stood shivering in front of the mirror while piles of shiny, slippery, form-fitting and flouncy dresses one size smaller than I would normally wear appeared like so many maniacal spring flowers above the door.

"It's going to be a classy wedding," I heard Mom tell Susan.

I tugged and slithered into a variety of dresses that crinkled like wrapping paper. I willed my body to compress, begged for larger sizes and less glam. Dutifully, I stepped outside the change room, where my mother poked, prodded, straightened my shoulders, glared into the mirror behind me. "You're puffy," she said. I slumped. "Stand up straight." A refrain from my childhood. I was fifty-five years old, and chastened. I could have stopped it. I'd learned long ago how to put a stop to it. But I didn't.

After an hour or so we gave up, and while I pulled on my Lycra jeans, I heard Mom outside the change room. "You should have seen her last summer. She had a nice little figure, because she had to work like a dog in the garden at their new house. Physical work, you know how that is."

On the way home in the car, I told her it was okay, that I would find something. We stopped to buy cherry Danishes, one of the only things she'd eat in those last couple years, though she'd once had a hearty appetite.

When I dropped her at the house, I watched her walk up the stairs to the front door before I backed out the drive. Her thinness, the hesitancy in each step, how tight-fisted her hand was on the railing revealed what she tried so hard to conceal, maybe had her entire life. My indestructible mother was on the brink of breakage, shrinking down to size zero: disappearing. Nothing in her favourite store fit her any longer, but she had hoped it might fit me, and I can't blame her for wanting to leave behind something of herself.

I now know not only the wounds a mother can inflict on a daughter but also the wounds a daughter can inflict on a mother. I know what it means to love a child who's not in your image, but in their own, and I now know what it means to love defencelessly, as my mother did.

My mother pushed against life as if she were the wind and life were the tide: the sheer hours of cleaning and working and cooking and shopping and bettering. But what could I possibly know as daughter except to use her as a reference point for myself, how I both wanted and didn't want to live my life. I wanted her physical strength, the force with which she moved her body through a house after a day on her feet at work. I wanted her wrath when it was time for wrath, her outrage when one of hers was hurting. My enemies became her enemies, and that's when I felt most loved, when she riled against those who hurt me. And though she paid for it, how she would shout at my father; that one time he slapped me, and for me, she slapped him back. I could use, maybe I do use, that kind of righteous wrath. I wanted her looks, badly, and because I believed I had to do the same, I wanted her sheer determination to be better than where she came from.

# LEARNING TO SWIM

I churned the water into a frenzy with my limbs and feet, fisting my tiny hands and punching forward and backward, my head held high above the lake's surface. I was six years old, exuberant with my newfound buoyancy and surprised by my body's capacity. "Watch me," I shouted at my four-year-old brother Russ while I demonstrated a dog paddle the way my mother had shown me.

On the sandy shore not far from us, my parents were seated on a blanket with my older brother and another couple, friends of the family. It was 1962, our last year in the north. Throughout my childhood, my family spent many summer hours alongside rivers, lakes and ocean beaches where my mother taught my siblings and me to swim. Likely, we'd driven out to this lake—somewhere near Prince George—on a Sunday. Let's say my father, big talker that he's always been, was engrossed in a conversation with his friend. My mother, whose belly was swollen with my younger sister, sat watching the woman, nodding her head in sympathy. For a moment, maybe a few brief moments, she averted her eyes from her children—not that I would have seen any of this at the time. When you're six, you assume your mother is always watching.

Russ, not taking his lesson seriously, spat a ribbon of lake water in my direction then collapsed backward in a fit of giggles. I lunged for him, and he palmed a wall of water into my face. Screeching, I flipped onto my stomach and paddled toward the raft that floated in the middle of the roped-off swimming area. My body slid through the water, as nimble as a fish; it was the first time I'd swum this far without my mother. A girl older than me lay on her belly on the warm planks, and a boy pushed another boy into the lake. Surrounded by laughter, scrambling limbs and splashing water, I pulled myself onto the raft and stood with the swagger of someone who'd gained membership in a private club. My muscles were charged with energy. "Look at me," I shouted to my parents, but through the throngs of children splashing in the shallows along the shoreline, they wouldn't have heard.

*Don't go over your head. Don't let him out of sight.* My mother's voice from earlier that day shattered my bravado. I spotted my brother not far from the raft. His head disappeared beneath the lake's surface then re-appeared, waggling like a bobblehead—above and below the water. It was okay; he was swimming, and it was me who had taught him to swim. The silly fish was trying to make me laugh the way he always did—I loved my little brother. I shouted again to my parents: "Look at me."

My mother was now on her feet and bounding toward us. "Get him!" she screamed, and a dark cloud crossed the sun, a chill gripped my body.

I leapt into the lake and swam until my feet found the bottom and I could reach for my baby brother. A rush of air hit me as a giant bird in my mother's body whooshed above and enveloped my choking, sobbing brother into its wings. It became my mother again, and the sun reappeared from behind the cloud. Wailing, I held my arms up to her, and she swung her flattened palm hard across my cheek, so hard I collapsed beneath the surface of the lake.

..

I never spoke of this memory to my mother, never asked my brother if he recalled how I almost let him drown, never told him how at the time I hated him for what I thought of as a trick he'd played on me to win my mother's favour. Did I hope my silence would erase the event, and isn't this where shame grows? In the wordless regions where a mother miscalculates, averts her eyes at the wrong moment, feels she doesn't measure up but her daughter must. From that day onward, I began the task of the good daughter, the task of sharing with my mother the burden of her shame.

..

When we were children Russ called me *fat*, and I called him *stupid*. Once he poured a glass of milk over my head, and I swung a vacuum cleaner hose at his stomach, knocking the wind out of him. On the acreage where we lived until I was thirteen, we hid behind prickly blackberry hedges and ambushed one another. We gave each other bruises and scrapes and learned not to tell. We played dress-up and put on skits for my parents on the cement patio at the bottom of the stairs. We took turns wearing my mother's dangly costume jewelry, her hairpieces, my father's cork boots and hard hat. We slept in slippery sleeping bags on the front lawn beneath starry summer skies, and we looked for the shapes of fanged serpents and one-eyed monsters in the constellations, for blood-sucking bats in the large willow on the edge of the yard. As for my older brother, who was made to join us those nights, we told him to *shut up*. Russ said he was *a suck* and that he was adopted by our dad, Mom told him. It was true Mom told him things she didn't tell my older brother or me, or even my father, just as my father told me things he didn't tell my mother or my siblings, like how he thought my mother spoiled my younger brother, and how his sister didn't like her.

While our baby sister was cocooned and my oldest brother seemed to exist in his own universe beyond the family, Russ and I were middle children who circled within the orbit of my parent's discord, performing our family drama as if it were some ghostly burlesque. Russ with his silver-capped front tooth, beguiling hazel eyes and his quick naughty wit, who mouthed off at school, lied to my parents and came home drunk at fifteen. My father told him he was nothing, my mother told him he was a prince. While he sparked with the family's wild light and surface rage, I embodied its subterranean despair. I plodded in his shadow, got good marks, covered for him, lectured him, adored him.

By grade eleven he'd run away at least half a dozen times then he dropped out of school and moved from home for good: to Vancouver, Montreal, Vancouver, New York City, Toronto. When he was in Vancouver the first time, he'd come home to ask my mother for money, to boast to my father about the wealthy men he knew personally, to bait him into anger. It was around this time Russ came out as gay. My mother said it was a phase. My father said my brother would have an easier life if he chose women, and he felt that my mother spoiling my brother accounted for his poor choice.

..

On the phone, by email and when Russ was out for a visit, we mocked our parents, tallied lovers—he had more than me—and jobs—also more than me. We tallied our failures, too, and we tallied each other's successes.

He was twenty-eight in 1986 when he revealed in the middle of an argument on the phone that he'd been diagnosed with HIV. In the silence that immediately followed, the vast distance between his voice in Toronto and mine on the West Coast lengthened and kept lengthening into a phantasmic tunnel through which human voice was beyond reach.

"I don't believe you," I said. "You're saying it because you're angry."

"You're right, I lied. Forget it."

I didn't believe his retraction, but that was the end of any discussion about it until a couple years later when he was out for a visit, and I said, "How are you, I mean your health?" It was two in the morning, and we were well into our second bottle of wine.

Russ stared at me for a long, sad moment. "Honey, it doesn't go away."

..

One summer in the mid-nineties, I picked Russ up at the airport before driving him up island to our parents' place in Mesachie Lake. The way he could stride off a plane in an expensive sweater, grinning that gorgeous grin, and say "Hi, Honey" made me proud that it was me he was meeting, made me want to say "My brother" in the way my mother beamed when she introduced him as "My son."

At the luggage carousel we chattered over one another about Toronto's soul-sucking weather, my kids, his recent trip to Puerta Vallarta, my job and the courses he was taking at U of T. Eventually, the crowd around us dissipated, and we stood before a revolving empty carousel. He stopped speaking mid-sentence. "Where's my fucking bag?"

I shifted my eyes around the empty room. "Damn," I said.

"There's a thousand dollars' worth of drugs in my suitcase."

"Wow" was all that came out of my mouth.

"It's not like they're illegal." He rolled his eyes and strode toward the Air Canada desk.

"I know," I said, too quietly for him to hear. I'd done some research and learned that HIV was a retrovirus that efficiently attacked the immune system, and AZT was a relatively new drug that seemed to help prolong the life of those with HIV, but it was also the most expensive prescription drug in history. I thought I'd been preparing for what might happen to my brother, but looking back, I see that doing the research was a substitute for conversation, a way of keeping his illness academic.

We went to a nearby restaurant for lunch while waiting for his suitcase to arrive on the next flight from Toronto.

"Are you okay?" I asked as we read the menus. Of course he wasn't okay.

"I'm fine, the drugs are expensive, but I've got some insurance. Beer or wine?" He snapped his menu closed and grinned.

After picking up his bag on the way up island to my parents' house we laughed: his descriptions of a macabre neighbour who trapped him in the elevator to warn him about the dangers of electromagnetic waves, his two-day stint as a barista and a man who'd resurfaced in his life, G, a man he'd forgotten, but who'd apparently not forgotten him.

"He says he'll take care of me. He's got a good job. He's... normal."

"Go for it," I said.

"Are you kidding me? The guy's so dull I want to take furniture polish to him."

After the HIV diagnosis, Russ became voracious for experience. No-matter relationships, holidays to warm beaches, good food and wine, it was all fleeting. He was free from the burden of long-term planning. This was his surface, what drew people to him.

Shortly after I returned home from dropping him at my parents' house, he called. "Three days max. Mom is already ragging on me about wet towels. Does your towel get wet when you dry yourself? It's a normal thing, right? Dad wants me to buy a truck. What am I going to do with a fucking truck at Jarvis and Wellesley in downtown Toronto?"

He needed me laughing uproariously—then he'd be okay, at least for now—but I heard the voltage in his voice, how his anxiety sparked in the presence of my father, how quickly it could tip. I knew, though my parents didn't, about the prescriptions—not the AZT, but the ones that buoyed him up, his "happy pills," as he called them. The family's volatility, how it leapt between my brother's synapses.

That same night at three a.m., I stumbled out of bed to banging on the front door. Russ, with my mother at his heels, strode into the house. There'd been a drama, some horrific scene between my father and brother. Versions of this occurred now and then, but it had been several years. Mom hung their jackets then offered to make tea, as if it were a regular visit. The house was sticky with August heat.

"What happened?" I asked.

Russ shook his head. "She's not going back there."

"What did he do to her?"

My mother returned with teacups and said, "He can't talk to your brother like that. It's been going on too long. Tell your sister what he called you." She sat next to him, rested her hand on his arm.

"Nothing I haven't been called before. It's how he talks down to you, Mom," said Russ.

Sometimes I thought my brother needled him to make my father an enemy so that he could be my mother's hero. But I also knew Russ didn't manoeuvre around my father's simmering condemnations, his triggers, the way the rest of us did, so other times I saw my brother's provocations as an act of courage.

"I should have left him years ago," my mother said. It might have been the late hour, but it felt as if we were actors in a play. Why now would she go along with this rescue mission, and why would Russ take it this far? And it came back to me, that suitcase full of drugs, the precarious chemical balance that held my brother together—for how long?

Russ rehashed the story of the blow-up with my father until he was able to turn it into parody, doing what he always did with his pain, transforming it to the gothic. I laughed with my mother, and it felt good to be sitting there. I went to the kitchen and made popcorn.

"We'll find her a nice little condo," said Russ. He didn't have the money, and I was a single parent working as an outreach counsellor for a non-profit. Regardless, as the light spread outside the living room window and traffic thickened on the thoroughfare in front of the house, he and I discussed neighbourhoods, imagined our mother without our father. He said she would have "nice things" for the first time in her life, and we would take her for dinners. We would take care of her, we said, and our voices got more and more excited as we spun scenarios, and she wrapped herself in a blanket and dozed like a child listening to a bedtime story.

When the children got up for school, they talked over one another competing for their uncle's attention. They begged him to stay on for a few days, to take them out for french fries. He rolled his eyes and sighed, feigning bored resignation to their request. "So spoiled," he said, "you always get what you want," then he walked them to school. After making breakfast for all of us, my mother drove home to my father.

..

I regret that G didn't save the blank journals I sent Russ, so I could know if he ever filled them, so I could finally learn something of my brother's deepest thoughts. That he would have filled those journals may have been a fantasy, but what comfort it would have been to hold in my hands the empty books and to imagine how he might have filled them.

I lost so many of his emails through the years; I read and read again the ones I was able to retrieve, especially those from the last few years of his life.

*December 13, 2003—Our intimate gathering of my closest friends for Christmas day dinner has turned into a larger event, complete with a number of arrogant, pretentious and exceptionally unfriendly Torontonians. Are you going to your beach house for Christmas? I would absolutely love to spend a few days up there.*

*January 31, 2004—It made me sad when you and T [our younger sister] took Mom to Tucson and Mom said it was the nicest place she had ever been. Now I'm older, I start to think of Mom like a little girl.*

*March 16, 2005—G just said he wants to be single. I guess he thinks being in your 50s and single is really fun. Once again, I will move. I'm leaning toward staying in Toronto and finishing my degree. I looked at some filthy and horrible apartments in my price range today... I may just load up my Dodge Colt and head west.*

*April 26, 2005—I used to always wonder what kind of a loser would live right beside a huge, busy highway....... as I now sit in my new box perched 18 stories above 10 lanes of traffic thundering by on one of Canada's busiest expressways, the Don Valley Parkway... Yes, Judy, I did talk to a lawyer. I was bought out, end of story.*

*October 14, 2005—Winter is looming. I want out of here.*

When I opened the door to him in November 2005, he forced a smile. His beautiful eyes were sunk deep in their sockets, and beneath my hug, I felt his skeleton.

Determined to purchase his own house for the first time in his life, he pored over Vancouver Island real estate papers and arranged appointments with agents. Home ownership was what you did in my family to make our parents proud.

In the end, all he could afford was a townhouse in Port Alberni, a small mill town nestled between the mountains on an inlet that wound its way to the west coast. Port, as it was known to those who'd been raised there and got away, was considered the armpit of Vancouver Island at that time. He wasn't an underemployed millworker, an unemployed logger, a kayaker or a hiker, nor a tree hugger. They'd eat my brother alive there for what he was not.

He moved into his place on May 1, 2006. A week later, he was hospitalized. I was away kayaking for the weekend, and my father called me at the lodge where my husband and I were staying.

"Liver cancer?" I'd asked my brother months earlier, when he'd let it drop in the middle of an email argument that he was dying. Research had told me my brother's liver could be failing from years of AZT and Hep C. He wouldn't talk about it, not to me, my mother or my sister, and most certainly not to my father. He was angry at me so often in those months since he'd arrived from Toronto. It didn't take much, and when I wasn't on the defensive, I didn't know what to believe. All of us said later we didn't know how sick he was. Can you ever really know?

I called G in Toronto, said "I thought you should know." G flew out and spent two weeks with Russ in his new townhouse when he was discharged. I drove up island from Victoria whenever I could. After two weeks, he was back in the hospital. Mom and I moved into his bedroom at the townhouse and G slept on the couch.

All day at the hospital we hovered at my brother's bedside while he drifted in and out of consciousness, and Mom cleaned around him, urged water on him until he could no longer drink, sponged his face, stroked his hands and rubbed his feet, while I talked about anything I could think of and apologized over and over for the arguments, all the stupid arguments. In the late afternoon Mom dozed in the chair, and I wandered on the grounds of the hospital wondering how this tiny mill town could possibly be my magnificent brother's final landing place. The hospital sat on a hill surrounded by a thick coniferous woods, and beyond, there were glimpses of the mountains and the sea. Here, this landscape, this west coast, was my home, and also his, always his, no matter how many years he'd lived away.

G relieved Mom and me in the evenings. Back at Russ's townhouse, we sat on my brother's newly purchased porch while she smoked, and we both drank beer.

"That nurse, you know the one on today," I said.

My mother nodded.

"She said 'You can swab his lips. You won't get *it*. Like I don't know how it's transmitted." I emphasized the word *it* in the way my brother would have had he been telling the story.

Mom shook her head. "Don't let it bother you. I've got shoes older than her."

I laughed. "She's a hick from Port." My voice pitched upward, unnaturally. It was the sort of thing my brother would say. Slick with a tinge of cruelty. It felt good on my tongue.

"Dumb as that stupid dog of yours."

"Dumber." I was really laughing now, and so was my mother, chortling and coughing, something approaching hysteria.

It would never be the same, the three of us, my brother, my mom; how happy I was to be the third wheel just so I could be in their company, the way we could lampoon any tragedy. We'd try, Mom and me, but it would never be the same.

I sighed and took a sip of warm beer while Mom butted her cigarette into the little tin can with the lid she carried everywhere.

"She's doing her best," she said.

'Who?"

"That little nurse, the one who said you wouldn't get it."

"I know."

"That's all you can do is your best, based on what you know at the time. It's never enough." My mother gazed out over the darkening sky. The firs loomed around the townhouse complex; frogs croaked somewhere down by the creek. The evening had cooled off, and I said we should go in.

On that last day, May 18, 2006, the nurse gave my mother a sedative, and we left the hospital when G showed up. I didn't ask him where he went all day, but I knew he took time to shower and to press a clean shirt every morning. He reeked of aftershave. And this irritated me.

"I've got to get Mom to bed. She's not been sleeping. Call me if this is the night. I want to be here when he dies," I said.

"I'll stay all night tonight," he said.

At three a.m., the door to the townhouse opened, and the lamplight washed into the bedroom. Mom stirred and opened her eyes beside me on the bed. I got up and went into the living room. G kicked off his shoes and stepped in my direction. "He's gone," he said.

A chill gripped me, the way it does when a black cloud crosses the sun. G reached forward with his fingers, touched my neck. His skin was clammy. "I'm giving you the last of his warmth. This from his neck." My smart beautiful brother would never say anything so stupid, so flaky. I flinched at his touch and turned to go to my mother.

She was on her back staring at the ceiling, her arms folded across her chest.

"Gone?" she asked.

"Yes." I crawled in beside her, and I'm not sure who took whose hand first. We lay like that with our eyes wide open until dawn, saying nothing.

# ELECTION DAY

My first ever visit to the home of my eighty-five-year-old uncle happened to coincide with the day of the 2019 federal election, so in my mind the two are conjoined. Since my husband and I were going to be in Squamish to visit friends, I decided to use it as an opportunity to finally get some answers about my Indigenous ancestry. As my mother's older brother, and the one in the family who was closest to my grandmother, I felt my uncle might be best able to reveal the family history of which, despite my efforts, I remained ignorant. Much of what I knew I'd gleaned from fragments of memory, threads of family conversations and reading between the lines, and from Ancestry.ca, Newspapers.com and other archives. I was frustrated with the roadblocks I'd come up against: the missing documents, including my grandmother's birth record, any information about where she attended school, my mother's birth certificate. Then there was all the reading I was doing about colonialist practice. The more I learned about assimilationist policies the more despair I felt at the conditions that led to the erasure of the Indigenous side of our family history. I was beginning to understand that though we were spared in many ways compared to others, my family counted as one of the many that had been at the mercy of unrelenting political forces.

After departing from our friends, with whom the election had been percolating beneath every conversation, my husband and I drive past candidate signs to my uncle's house while voices on CBC rattle with commentary on expected outcomes. His three-bedroom bungalow is neat inside and out. Mom always said he looked after his place. At the door he greets me with "Hi, Jude," and I recall how fond I've always been of him, though we've seen so little of one another over the years. We hug and he invites us into the kitchen. The fluorescent kitchen light creases and washes out his once-handsome face, lands on a full head of hair, slicked back, the way he's always worn it, its ebony shine faded to grey. We chat about the ferry ride from the island, the drive, how much Squamish has changed. There's no mention of the election, and for the few hours we sit at my uncle's kitchen table, we're free of its intrusion.

My call must seem out of the blue to my uncle, this niece who's driven past the road to his house for years to stay in the expensive condos on the Whistler ski hill and never once, not once dropped in for a visit. Despite that, I can tell he's pleased I'm here. I like to think I was the favourite of his sister's children. The last time I'd seen him had been in my mother's room in the palliative care unit of the Nanaimo General Hospital, days away from her death in 2015. She'd been barely conscious, and when my uncle appeared in the doorway, my auntie, the youngest sister, who was on constant watch, nodded at her brother and took my mother's hand. "Guess who's here," she said. My uncle leaned over the bed. "Hello, Honey." At the sound of his voice, Mom's eyes fluttered open, and her mouth twitched toward a smile.

Uncle sips his coffee then tells me he's got a story about horseback riding on their uncle's ranch near Clinton. "Your mom, she always had to beat me." He grins.

"Mom loved horses." When I say this, I realize I don't know what I'm basing it on. Sometimes she'd say there were horses on her father's brother's ranch. I only saw her on a horse once, when my sister and I took her on a holiday to a resort in Tucson for her sixty-fifth birthday, where we went trail riding. She'd sat so naturally on the wide back of the animal you'd think nothing in that hot, dry landscape could topple her.

"So, we're on Uncle Buster's horses," says Uncle. "They were big guys. She's racing ahead of me. I never cared if she beat me, so I'm just trotting along. She gallops out of sight then finally I get to a gate, no sign of your mom, but her horse is standing there with an empty saddle, snorting like he's got something important on his mind. I get closer and see your mom's sitting on her ass on the other side of the gate in the mud, mad as hell." He chuckles and his eyes light up. He's replayed this memory how many times?

"Wow. What'd she do?" I ask.

He shrugs. "She gets up, opens the gate, jumps on the horse and off she goes. Damned determined to beat me. That was your mom." He nods, the smile drifting from his face, eyes cast toward the grey day outside the window.

"She was tough," I say.

"She was rough and feminine at the same time."

Growing up I heard more than once that my mother was "a lady." Sometimes it was as if people were surprised by her insistence on manners, the way she held her head high, the neatness of her house and her dress.

My mother married my father, a white man without a trace of Indigenous blood, and after several years of struggle they bought not a horse, but a boat—did she ever tell him that it was a horse she wanted?—and cruised amongst the Gulf Islands. Sometimes they went to Friday Harbor on San Juan Island. Not once did she mention that her mother was born on that island or that her grandparents had farmed there for twenty years. As if there was a gate she had to clear to shake off the memory of a past she never knew, my mother couldn't get far enough away from where she came.

"She was a worker," my uncle says, the highest compliment in my mother's family. I don't remember a time she didn't work outside the house as well as inside: store clerk, meat wrapper, upgrading and college courses so that she could become a medical receptionist, and in her retirement her own little garden shop; and at the end of the workday, the washing, ironing, scrubbing with bleach and cooking for four kids and my father.

He gets to his feet and shuffles to the coffee machine, waving away my insistence that I'll get it for him.

"I don't eat much in the way of sweets," he'd shouted into the phone earlier that day. "You don't have to bring nothing, Jude."

His hearing is not so good, but he's wiry and strong, rakes his own leaves, and has lived solo since his third wife died several years before. Auntie says this last wife was his one true love.

He sits down and spreads photos across the table.

..

One year after our visit, I pause before calling my uncle. In this ongoing pursuit of family history, am I abusing the good will between us to get him to talk? *Did my grandmother ever go to residential school? Did my great-grandmother ever sing in SENĆOŦEN to her children, her grandchildren? How many ways were you and my mother told it was better to pass for white?* I've not asked him these questions, the echo of taboo running deep in my own blood. And yet, he's the oldest in the family, the last of two surviving siblings, and known for his good memory—which he'll take with him when he dies.

..

Before the visit to my uncle's, Auntie warned me about mentioning the "Native stuff" to her brother. "He doesn't want to talk about it," she said, "even though he looks Native, and half his friends are Indians." Several years ago, she joined a First Nations drumming group with the Quw'utsun, who are across the inlet from the W̱SÁNEĆ and with whom we have many kinship ties. I have vague childhood memories of meeting relatives from both sides of the inlet. Auntie tells me bits of gossip she hears about cousins and great-aunties, many of whom I've never known, and in my mind, I sketch it all into the family tree, try to keep it straight.

She's the only one in my mother's family who freely admits to these connections. "I look more Indian than most of them," she says, her compact body shaking with laughter. She says "them" as if she's the outsider or as if they are the outsiders. She doesn't say "us." These days she spends most of her time alone in her small apartment. The drums hang on the wall, and she wants to give them to my grandchildren, her sister's great-grandsons, two blue-eyed boys far removed from their great-grandmother's history.

..

At my uncle's house, I see for the first time a photo of my great-grandmother.

"Rosalie?" I ask, smiling.

"I'm pretty sure that's her, Jude."

A chubby-faced woman with an ample lap on which sits a baby about a year old is seated on a blanket in what appears to be a stubbled field. A wagon wheel behind her head fills a corner of the picture. The image is black and white, grainy; it's an old photo.

She appears middle-aged or older, her face lined. I know from my research, but don't say, that she's been through a lot by the time of this photo: the birth of ten children and death of at least two, a move from Saanich to San Juan Island to Squamish, a husband's debilitating accident. Then there was all that was not articulated in the space between official records.

"San Juan Island?" I ask without taking my eyes off the photo.

"No, that'd be after, across the street there, where I was born." He flicks his thumb in the direction of the window and explains that the suburb immediately around his house was once farmland owned by my great-grandparents. My grandparents lived with them until they built a house for themselves on the property where my mother would have lived when she was a baby.

This is news to me. For the first time, I'm able to position my mother in a time and location where she experienced a childhood, and so too am I able to add at least a fragment of linearity to my own history.

"You live across the street from where you were born?"

"You betcha, Jude. I tried to leave once. Worked over there on the island, same place as your dad, in the bush, you know, always worked in the bush. But I came back after a year." He struggles to his feet and gets another coffee, waves my husband away when he offers to get it for him.

"Who's the baby?" I ask.

My uncle examines the picture and shrugs.

"Mom?"

"Could be." He nods, raises his eyebrows. He wants to make this into memory for me. My husband snaps a photo of the photo with his phone and annoyance flitters across Uncle's brow.

My great-grandmother smiles into the camera beneath a hat encircled with flowers. Attached to the back of the hat a soft white veil appears to unfurl from her shoulders in the shape of wings. In fact, there's something ethereal about the photo, the grandmother and child dressed in white, the child in a long gown as if they've just come from a christening, as if enclosed in wings that hover above the stubble of a half-ploughed field. The small fingers of the child, whom I've decided is my mother, grasp the woman's hand. I'm imagining my mother in the warmth of that abundant lap, and on the morning the photo was taken she was blessed. Such a look of contentment in her grandmother's smile, as if she has every little thing she needs:

this grandchild, the sun on her bare arm, the smell of the fertile earth, the sound of the river, her husband's plough and horses resting nearby, the murmuring of children on the grass, laughter—there must have been laughter.

Quite possibly the baby in the photo wasn't my mother, and my great-grandmother may have been sitting there in arthritic pain, just as her grandson, my uncle, would on the day many years later when I first laid eyes on the photo. She might have felt exhaustion and resentment for her daughter, my grandmother, who'd left the child in her care. But this is not what I want for my great-grandmother, for my grandmother or my mother. Let me impute a history where there was no known history, one that doesn't hurt. Marianne Hirsch, author and Columbia University professor introduced the concept of "postmemory." She says that family photographs become like portals into a disrupted, fractured past through which descendants produce a pseudo memory that is as close to actual memory as is available to them. Post generations are driven by "the desire to repair" the suffering inflicted on their ancestors. Hirsch refers specifically to the offspring of Holocaust survivors, but her work has been applied to a range of historical traumas, such as those experienced by Indigenous people. In the lexicon of the day my grandmother would have been a "half-breed" with parents who each also would have been considered the same. It was understood in the way it is in families that my grandmother folded the half we didn't talk about into her shadow as if it were a dark-eyed, disgraced daughter.

Out of all her children her oldest son, my uncle, was her favourite, and his favoured position in the family came with a burden of loyalty. He refused to go with Auntie when she drove up to Squamish to drum over their mother's grave in honour of what would have been my grandmother's hundredth birthday. My mother also refused to go with her, so my auntie took her two adult children, a Quw'utsun drum and an old boombox with a cassette tape on which a Quw'utsun acquaintance had recorded a Hul'q'umi'num' honour song, as it was not a song Auntie knew by heart.

"Those songs are hard to learn," she said years afterwards, when she described the event to me. She and my cousins had stood above my grandmother's grave in the deserted cemetery at Brackendale while she beat on the drum to the accompaniment of the scratchy recording in the way she'd been taught by near-strangers with nebulous kin connections.

"Then I felt it," she said, "my mother's bones rattling in the earth. Like an electric shock going through me." At the same time, one of my cousins saw rising mist at the periphery of her vision. She watched it resolve into the shape of people drifting between the trees at the edge of the forest. She knew it had to be the ancestors and she told her mother later that their presence was comforting, a confirmation that she, her brother and her mother were not imposters. Meanwhile, down the road my uncle sat at his kitchen table drinking a beer and feeling an old familiar shame. And a ferry ride and several kilometres away my mother dug deeper and harder into her garden.

Some might accuse my auntie of cultural misappropriation, some of revenge, given how vehemently her mother denied her Indigenous heritage and given the difficult relationship my mother and she had with their mother, who would label them "dirty Siwash" when she was angry. Some, like my father and uncle, would dismiss it as superstition. I choose to see it as Auntie did, a way to bridge the past and present, non-history and history, silence and voice. According to Hirsch, Auntie's ceremony would be an example of taking the present into the past in order to rewrite the history, to acknowledge the unacknowledged: a reconstruction.

..

On our way out of my uncle's house we go through the attached garage where the walls are lined with elk and deer antlers of various sizes. I tell him Mom showed me the newspaper article about him winning the lottery for that big elk, something he'd dreamed of all his life. He shifts his eyes away then back, a flash of defiance like I've seen in my mother's eyes. He doesn't own a computer, isn't on Facebook or Instagram or Twitter, but he knows how people feel about hunting. He knows this niece who's never been to his house before is university educated and married to a university-educated guy who works in an office. In his world men who work in offices aren't to be trusted. I understand where he's coming from in a way my husband doesn't.

"I only got quality meat. I'd go way up the mountains; not like they hunt now. I'd go on my own two feet and be gone for months at a time. These mountains were different then, not so logged. Had to go every damn year. The boss would tell me if I went, they'd fire me, and I'd say, 'That's okay, you'll hire me back.'" He pauses and his handsome face flashes a smile. "And they always did."

We laugh and pull on our coats, chat about the ferry, and he reassures us we'll make it in time. I don't tell him we have one more stop to make before we head there. My husband opens the door and steps outside. I hug Uncle's sinewy shoulders. He's thin and tough and tender-hearted like my mother was, like she had to be.

My husband is in the carport checking his phone, and I turn toward him with my back to Uncle.

Behind me, his voice is hushed. "They were from respected tribes, your great-grandparents," Uncle says. "Respected and rich."

I look over my shoulder and nod. I know not to press him, that this is as much as he can give, and that it has been modified to make it a narrative with which he can live.

"Don't you forget it, Jude."

"I won't," I say.

..

The sky above the cemetery is bloated with rain and the trees amongst which my cousin saw the ancestors are motionless. I step between the small concrete slabs that lay flat on the rain-soaked grass, not sure whether I'm walking on or between the graves. Mats of soggy leaves cover several of the stones. Though no one actually knows where they're buried, I imagine my great-grandparents beneath that ground, their names worn away. My husband has organized himself into a methodical hurried search for my grandmother's marked grave, up one row and down the other, while I wander, directionless.

A weight presses on me, and I stop above a stone covered in leaves except for the word Pearl. My grandmother's name. I crouch down and brush the leaves aside.

*Pearl Mildred McKee*
*Forever loved by her husband and family*
*1911–1973*

When I think of her, I recall cat's-eye spectacles that concealed her eyes, a hand clutching a narrow-necked bottle of beer. Her husband, her third, had the look of a hound dog with great folds of white skin around his neck and a bald head. The rare times she came around, my mother shrunk in her presence, while my father swelled as if to remind my grandmother that my mother was now all his to improve. Dad told me recently that my mother "wanted to put herself above it."

"What's the *it*?" I asked.

He hesitated. "Her... her... environment."

It's not what he meant; he meant that her marrying him had saved her from her past, the *Indian in her*, though he'd learned not to say so, and not to say *Indian*. My father was only enacting on a microcosmic level the policies an assimilationist culture implemented on a macro level. Every family is its own state, has its own political agenda.

In that moment above her grave, I ache to hear my grandmother's voice and to know what I will never know about her life, how her story became my mother's story and how now my mother's story is mine. Now that she is long dead, I want to believe it's a story she can finally tell. A story my mother, also now dead, can finally hear.

I half-expect to see my grandmother as a girl with long black hair and warm brown eyes emerge from the shadows, drift like a milky disc of light between the trees, but only dusk's shadows blur the edge of the cemetery.

..

The highway winds under the low clouds and gusts of rain, and out the car window I catch glimpses of blue mountains and the sea far below. "This coastline, the mountains..." I shake my head at the beauty. My husband's attention is on the road. Though I've been up and down the Sea to Sky over the years with cars full of noisy kids and friends, I've never really seen it in the same way. What would it have been like before the highway?

"When your parents moved back to Squamish for those few years, when you were a baby, they would have had to take a ferry. No highway then," my uncle had said.

I search my body, somewhere in my DNA maybe, for a twinge of recognition.

With one hand on the steering wheel my husband reaches with the other for the radio controls. He wants news of the election. Voices crackle through static. Based on what we can hear, we aren't so much pleased as resigned to the fact that the party that's in the lead, even if it isn't our preferred party, is better than the other party we feared might win.

Traffic thickens as we get closer to the ferry terminal, and rain slivers the gathering dusk. We line up beneath a cliff face. Unable to see beyond rows of cars, anxiety jitters my thoughts as it sometimes does waiting for ferries—fear that we're in the wrong lineup and we have no idea where we're headed. Out the steamy car window I watch my husband disappear across the lot into the grey light.

Once aboard, we eat burgers and scroll through our phones in the ferry cafeteria. The results are coming in on a TV near where we sit. Several passengers cluster around the screen. I tell my husband that our candidate is in the lead in our riding. He nods without looking up from his phone. He's done some door knocking, and he plans to drive in to the party headquarters when we get home. Rain whips at the ferry windows. The party headquarters are housed in a cramped office with bright overhead lights. I imagine the weary faces, the orchestrated cheers, the TV camera. The chill. I tell him he can go without me.

To my husband politics is about affiliation, a team sport, and it's about moral indignation at inequity and injustice. He has faith in a system that he believes represents the will of the people. These days, politics is something I'd like to peel off me as if it were a skin in need of shedding. At the same time, I'm haunted by the Truth and Reconciliation Commission's report on residential schools, the report on murdered and missing women, and a recent report on widespread and systemic racism against Indigenous people in BC's health care system. Another study. I'm weary to the bone, as are my ancestors. I can feel it in my blood, the political machinations that decide what goes underground, decade after decade. And yet, this day, after the visit with my uncle, I know it's not the whole story. In my uncle's house it was as if there was no election. He has his house where he's lived most of his life, on the land he was born to amongst the mountains, in a place where he spent many of his winters doing what he loved best. He has his albums full of family photos tucked into the cabinet under the television. "I've got lots more, Jude," he said. "I'll show you next time you come." My uncle refuses to participate in a system that would insist he stood on one side or the other, that would ensure his marginal status for the Indigenous in him, or on the other hand, deem him untrustworthy for his whiteness. He's learned to live alongside such a system, to resist in his own quiet standoff.

The next day, I'm rested and glad to be back after so many days away. I'm getting more like my uncle, more fixed to the place I call home. All morning voices on the radio rattle with reactions to the election.

The rain has stopped, and the sun burns through the fog along the shore. Out on the beach, the dog and I sniff the clear air. A seal pushes his bulk through the water and a kingfisher chatters and dives above our heads. Only a few weeks earlier I swam off this shore, and now I wear a toque, a Cowichan toque with an eagle design, something Auntie gave me. She knows the Hul'q'umi'num' woman who made it for me.

There are maps all over Facebook, the country divided by different colours, delineating the divisions between the parties, the division in the country.

My feet shuffle through maple leaves along the path. Amongst the colour and light and cool clean air, I imagine the forest is free of politics. But in minutes the trail winds out of the trees and along the dike, and above me the highway clear-cuts scar the mountainsides like raw sores.

A man appears with a dog on a leash. Is he one of the locals who are against dogs running free? I call my dog and dangle his leash as if I'm about to attach it to his collar. I don't want trouble. The man hollers, "It's okay," and unleashes his dog. He calls him a "doofus" and we laugh. I see we're on the same side.

..

It's now a year since the visit with my uncle, and there's still so much I don't know, may never know. I tap his number into my phone and imagine him in his bungalow across the strait amongst the north shore mountains. It rings several times and goes to the answering machine.

"Hi, Uncle, it's your niece. It's been a while since we talked, but I'm thinking about you and..."

"Hi there, Honey, sorry, I was just out back." He's breathless.

We talk about the damn leaves piling up, how he still rakes them himself, and the rain. No snow yet.

"Never any over here on the island."

"That's what they all say." He chuckles. "God's country, right?"

"Maybe it snows now and then."

"I know. You're just bugging me."

We chat a few more minutes and he tells me about his daughter's recent visit, my cousin, who I haven't seen since we were children. I don't tell him she hasn't returned my calls, and Auntie thinks it may be because of the falling out Auntie has had with Uncle, a loyalty issue, or was it because my cousin heard I was snooping around with an aim to uncover long-buried family history. At this, I'm afraid I've failed, and the stories of my ancestors will remain buried. I've come up against the wall, against memory, or maybe it's more like what Russian author Maria Stepanova describes in *Memory of Memory*, in that a family's past, particularly where traumatic historical events have occurred, is at best non-linear, half hidden, a book of scraps. I don't press my uncle for more because like Stepanova "I am so scared of hurting these people because I feel it in myself, a sense of hurt, a blood link and a proximity with each of them, all those who hid their Jewishness like an embarrassing defect." The word "Indigeneity" could fit in there, too.

..

I had a crush on my uncle when I was a child, his warm brown eyes and even temperament, how Mom's happiness spread around the house when her beloved brother came to visit, how their banter would fall easily into sync—the case of Lucky Lager beer always at his feet the only tension between them. It was like my mother was grounded when he was there and so was I, as if we knew for a brief few hours from what ground we came. Or if this memory is a reconstruction, something I can live with, let it be that. This is how I choose to remember.

# HOUSE IS NARRATIVE

Alice Munro says a story is like a house. "You can go back again and again, and the house, the story, always contains more than you saw the last time. It also has a sturdy sense of itself of being built out of its own necessity, not just to shelter or beguile you."

..

From my vantage point on the stairs of the community hall where I once was a Brownie then a Guide, I search for the house of my childhood across the two lanes of Herd Road, a few kilometres out of Duncan. If it's still there, it's now shrouded by a line of shrubs tangled with blackberry, branches brittle and criss-crossed, some mere sawn-off trunks revealing nothing of what's behind them.

When I was a child, the house was exposed to the road, its green lawn sloping into a ditch in which my brothers and I scavenged for blunt beer bottles on Sunday mornings, tossed from passing cars the night before.

I've parked to the side of the hall in front of the tennis court. We were sixties kids, late baby boomer, working class; we were told we could be anything we wanted. For boys, this meant an astronaut or an engineer; for girls, a nurse or maybe a movie star. It was my father who wanted to name me after Judy Garland. One day we could all have a tennis court of our own. I remember the excitement in the neighbourhood when one was built at the community hall. My mother quickly signed up my older brother and me for lessons.

Chicken wire has been jimmied across an opening where a chain-linked door once stood. Inside the walls of the court grass grows through the cracks in the pavement and three bicycles loll at random on their sides, one missing a tire. The net is also missing.

Houses are aspirational in nature in that they yearn for improvement. Time passes, stairs sag, paint fades, floors wear. They can never be exactly as they were, and they want to be better than their original conception. Memory is like that. It doesn't want to restore so much as renovate, to see anew.

..

My brother and I are on one side of the net and on the other is a tall, lanky, pimple-faced kid who was held back at school. A scrapper. He has in his hand a tennis racket. Likely, it's mine. He's playing against my brother—though they aren't really playing, just clobbering the ball across the net. My brother keeps missing the tall kid's serves. My mouth is moving, words arrowed at this kid, and I'm leaping about. He thinks he's tough, better than my brother, this boy. He stops, swings the racket over his shoulder like a rifle, strolls in my direction, towers over me. When he speaks, he barely moves his mouth. "If you don't shut up, I'm going to shut you up."

In a gesture of precise mimicry, as if my mouth is a switch he's flipped, out of it pop gun the words he's just spoken. With the same mechanical precision, his fist makes contact with my teeth. We live in the same neighbourhood, this boy and me.

Behind us looms the mountain with its rocky crown and war memorial and the logging trucks howl on the road. Then it's me howling with a mouthful of pain and blood tracing my teeth, and I run home. My father is at the front of the house crouched on the ground with nails between his lips. He's finishing up a frame for the new stairs. He and Mom have the same frenetic energy for improvement. She's on the side of the house extending the garden. He listens to my story without looking up then takes the nails from his mouth and says, "Get in the car." My brother has skulked past my father, and the scrapper boy should be almost home.

I wait in the warm truck, the heat suffocating, while my father goes to talk to my mother. A few minutes later he jumps in, starts the engine and winds down the window. My mother stands by the stairs, her bottom lip caught by her teeth. She thinks to wave. On our way to the boy's place, my father asks me to tell him again what happened. The boy lives in a small house with two sagging cement steps leading to his front door. There are no trees on the property, only an overgrown lawn pockmarked with dandelions. We knock, and the boy's mother, a woman with a doughy face, answers the door. My father asks to speak to her husband.

"He's not home," she says.

My father tells her what happened and makes me open my mouth so he can show her the chipped teeth.

The woman rubs her dry hands together. "She shouldn't have been so mouthy."

On our way home in the truck, we don't talk. I'm to understand that this means he's in agreement with the woman. My mother says nothing but makes me hot chocolate before bed. The heat hurts my teeth. To this day my two top front incisors are serrated at the biting edge, marked with the memory of a fist.

..

Before getting in the car, I climb the stairs of the community centre once again and slowly scan the top of the messy hedge for a sign that the old house exists. Between the uppermost branches a dormer window emerges, for a second appearing as if it's not quite fixed on to anything, as if it free floats there in the mottled March sky.

..

Though it's midday, the sun slides behind the mountain, a whiff of dewy grass and skunk cabbage rises in the air, a chorus of frogs serenades the dusk and dim stars, and from across the road my mother's voice calls that it's time to come inside. I'm leaning against a tree with my hands over my eyes, and I'm counting to one hundred. I'm only at fifty. My brothers, the sisters from Somenos Road, the boy with the lisp and the boy with the swimming pool hide somewhere in the shrubbery that borders the community centre's playing field. My mother calls again.

..

The distance across the road from the community centre to the start of our drive was once immense, potholed and patched with asphalt. Traffic rushed like a turbulent river between where we stood and home. Today, it's a simple matter to cross between cars and walk toward the old house.

On the other side, I peek around the trees up the curved driveway. On my left a long, free-standing garage stands over a rocky outcropping once dominated by a giant fir that held a tree fort where my brothers and I pretended we were stranded on an island like the characters on *Gilligan's Island*. And straight ahead is a small building with a large deck into which is sunk a concrete pool.

We'd always wanted a pool, my brothers and me. My mother, too— she said, "Maybe one day." Gerald T.'s family had one, and I like to think that it was not this fact but his fair skin and blond mop that made him the object of my budding pubescent desire. It never went anywhere, but I enjoyed his pool, can still smell its chlorine.

A man in a red T-shirt pushes a long-handled net around the surface of the pool. Its deck is attached like an odd appendage to a house that now reveals itself as that of my childhood. Worn wooden shakes have replaced the stucco. The stairs of rough concrete are the same ones my father poured half a century ago. They lead up to a weathered grey porch, whitewashed in my parents' time. The garden beneath the dormer window, once colourful with my mother's flowers, is a weed patch.

It had always been a proud house, and now it radiates a tatterdemalion pride but finally has its swimming pool. The house's bulging bay windows at its front, two dormers raised above the roof, and its elegant circular drive prevail. Despite the rumble and exhaust stink from the highway, its three storeys stand tall.

A square-shouldered young woman with her hair swept into a ponytail and a child on her hip comes out the front door and onto the porch. Her inquiry is businesslike. I explain about this being my childhood home. My eyes drift upward beyond where she stands on the porch to a dormer window. Unlike the lower floors of the house, it retains the original stucco, a palimpsest insisting on its former self.

She sighs, relieved. "I thought you were here about the dog."

A mutt circles around my legs, his large jaw and rippled back suggesting that under different circumstances he might turn vicious. I scratch his ears. "No," I say, and she invites me in.

The woman likes the open arch that leads out of the hallway into the living room, the soft corner coves that transition from wall to ceiling, the deep bay windows against which I see in my mind the brocaded drapes of another era, and in front of them, a couch, its scratchy material still a sensation on my fingertips. A child, kneeling there years and years ago, head resting on its back, watches the road, waiting for her father to come home. Sometimes he doesn't, once for a whole year.

The woman says they chose this house because they prefer the older ones and that they have plans to renovate. She points to the fireplace. "Were the bricks always white?" she asks. I shrug.

One time my father brought home a gift from the logging camp he flew in to and out of every ten days. His duffle was still packed where he'd dropped it by the front door, and I could smell the diesel on him. He wore his suspenders, and after lighting a fire in the fireplace, he called my brothers, my younger sister and me over. From a paper bag he dug out a handful of sparkling granules and threw them on the fire. The fire blazed and out of the flames erupted a kaleidoscope of jabbing, dancing colour.

My father went into the woods and came out of the woods; I thought of it as a magic place, my father capable of wizardry. He didn't want us to be afraid of anything. Sometimes he would take us for drives high up on the logging roads, drive hard toward the edge of a steep incline, and stop. What my father didn't see, and nor did I until I became an adult, is that it was his own fear of failed brakes, of flailing out of control over the incline, he was trying to conquer. I grew up being afraid.

The gnarled cherry tree is framed in the window that faces the side yard. Though obviously grown, when I was small it seemed as big as I see it now. I taste its bitter chokecherries on my tongue. We spat the pits at one another, my brothers and me. Beneath it, only a few months ago, I saw my mother in a dream. It was winter and her garden was empty. With a shovel she dug into the heavy soil, her body young and muscled the way I remember it well into those aging years.

"What are you digging?" She wore only the blue sweatshirt she always wore in the garden. I hung off the back porch. I wanted her to come in out of the cold.

I have so few dreams of her, and when I do, I ask her questions that she doesn't answer.

The large TV over the fireplace is turned on to a children's cartoon. On a child's table sit two plastic plates mounded with macaroni and sliced apple. "A picnic," I say, and smile at the girl who is about eight or nine years old. She leads me into the kitchen where there's an island that wasn't there before. She points out the kitchen window to a place beyond the back porch.

"There used to be a playhouse, but it was falling apart," she says.

I nod. "My dad built that house." The ceiling was low, meant for kids only. He'd put a door on it and cut a window into two of the walls. We had a table in there like the one in the living room for the children. We played *Little House on the Prairie* and *The Beverly Hillbillies*. We pretended we had a swimming pool.

"My dad built a large attic bedroom upstairs for my brothers."

"There's two now, and a bathroom," says the woman.

Out the window, at the bottom of the grey stairs, grass grows through the cracks of a concrete patio.

..

The sun is warm, and my younger brother and I are barefoot, poised with long sticks. A white metal barrel rotates on a stand, its small motor churning. My father says we can carve the year into the concrete once he pours it into the frame. We want to stand on it when it's still wet, to make imprints of our feet, but my mother says no. She fills a box with my parents' old clothes, and all that summer we hold performances on the new patio with the neighbourhood kids. I wear a red dress with a string of fake pearls. My brother wears overlarge shiny black shoes. My parents sit on the stairs and clap enthusiastically.

..

The young woman sees me looking at the door that leads from the kitchen to the basement.

"It's still unfinished down there," she says.

"There was a darkroom, built before we moved in."

"Not now," shrugs the woman.

..

No windows and no ventilation, only a sink and shelves, a trace of sickly chemicals in the stale air. A space in which our young imaginations conjure illicit scientific experiments. We turn off the light and scream and scream above the anguished pitch of adult voices that spear downward through the ceiling tiles from upstairs. We scream louder.

A pronounced crash and glass shatters above us. My best friend and my brothers bolt from the darkroom and out the basement. I creep upstairs to find the kitchen table overturned with all its soiled dinner plates, encrusted cutlery and glasses, mashed potatoes, a pork chop left over and meant for tomorrow night's dinner, all of it on the floor, spilled, smashed into tiny bits of tableware. The Arborite table with its metallic edge shining, flat on its back, its legs sticking straight up in a gesture of surrender. A stillness in the room. My parents move about somewhere in the house, not speaking.

It's not the first time my father has done this, and it won't be the last. Some part of me shifts from another part, and I feel as if that part could defy gravity and float above the wreckage. It's a summer evening, dusk accumulating outside the kitchen window, everything broken on the floor surrounding the upturned table.

..

The door to the basement is closed; so too are the doors in the hallway where my parents' bedroom and the one I shared with my sister were located. Closed. The woman doesn't invite me upstairs.

In the narrative that is the house, some doors remain closed and what happens behind them generates the story.

"We have to hurry," the woman says. The girl watches me as if I am not quite real, a ghost. The woman places a hand on her shoulder. "We're going to get our Easter photos taken today."

"Lovely," I say. I'd forgotten about Easter. "The creek?"

"Yes, still there. It floods up the bank almost to the house now."

"I don't remember it doing that, but one year when it was cold enough my father made a skating rink down there for us."

She smiles and looks at her watch.

The kitchen door leads to the back porch. I think, unfortunately for the woman, it's the same door from my childhood, with its window of thin glass, how it would rattle in the wind, the cold that came through. I hope for her sake there's been a lock installed. Before we went out and at night before bed, my mother would slide a butter knife into the door jamb below the knob.

..

We're upstairs in the bedroom that Dad built for my brothers: my mother, my two brothers, my baby sister and me. The scent of fresh pine is strong from the wood panels newly installed beneath the slanted ceilings. Mom says to leave the light off and we see only by the remote stars through the dormer window. She unravels my sleepy younger sister from around her neck and folds her into my arms. She takes my younger brother's hand and guides him over to my older brother's bed, where she sits and pulls him on her lap. My older brother kneels beside her, his eyes, wide and shadowy in the dark room, fixed on me. Downstairs the glass in the kitchen door rattles again, and there's more pounding. My sister whimpers and I hold her closer until she drifts back to sleep, then I tuck her under the blankets.

My father is shouting and for a moment it's not language I hear rising through that flimsy door, along the hallway and up to the attic room he built, but his voice dissolving into the raucous cries of a bird, the sound a crow makes, dissolving into my memory; the word that arises half-human, half-crow, is "Squaw."

..

In the dream I have had most often about this house, I wander in a sub-base-ment that is unfamiliar. The dimly lit rooms go on and on. Some have fur-niture. Some have nothing but a bare floor. There are few details. I don't know at first where I am, but then the knowledge that I'm back in the house on Herd Road reaches my consciousness, and it seems so obvious. I won-der how I could not have known, as if I've always been there and always will be.

We moved from Herd Road when I was thirteen so it's as if the house itself—with its solid foundation, its good bones, darkroom and attic—con-tains the whole of my childhood. No, not contains, it's more that the house itself breathed and dreamed my childhood. Mom always said it was haunt-ed. When we lived there my sister had an imaginary friend who was so real she later wanted to look her up in the town's archives.

In Victoria, where we moved, we lived in a newer house in a suburb, one with a cathedral entrance. My father bought a cabin boat and we spent weekends on the ocean in the Saanich Inlet, where my mother's ancestors, the ones we rarely spoke of, lived for thousands of years. This was as close to a swimming pool my mother ever got.

The house of my childhood has outlived my mother and will outlive me. Its story will change with each renovation. With each new occupant, its own dreaming will shift and grow in the way of a story, in the way of retrospection. Its memory of itself, as memory does, will wobble, as will its floors. Its foundation will one day reach a conclusion.

# PEARL & STELLA

# Helix

I wake at night floundering for connections that aren't there and wonder why I'm doing it, writing any of this. She's been gone for seven years now, my mother. Not gone: dead. I've come to understand the difference. Also, how she left her DNA behind.

..

My great-great-grandmother ZIȻOT was full-blooded Straits Salish. Her marriage to a white blacksmith from Scotland in 1866 signalled the precise moment in which my matrilineal genome was fractured. This was nine years after the Gradual Civilization Act was passed, and was followed by the Gradual Enfranchisement Act of 1869, and these two acts not so gradually culminated in the Indian Act. The gist of this was, according to Bonita Lawrence, upon marriage to white men "...not only were [Indian] wives removed from inheritance rights and automatically enfranchised with their husbands, but Section 6 began a process of escalating gender discrimination that would not be definitively changed until 1985."

..

If I were an artist, I would construct a double helix out of brightly coloured plastic straws. It would take dexterity of hand, four different colours and a billion straws, those bendable ones, to depict the twisted ladder that is the DNA molecular structure.

..

I've resisted sending in a sample of my spit to AncestryDNA, but I've been poring over Section 6 of the Indian Act as if it could bring my mother back. I remind myself that those last years, especially, were so hard, and when she went, at least at first, I felt some relief for her and for those who watched her suffer. Then I find myself reaching for the phone to call her because I want to tell her some little thing.

..

It was Rosalind Franklin who made the initial discovery that led to an understanding of DNA in the 1950s, but it was three men who received the Nobel Prize for it in 1962. There's no direct link to my mother's experience here except that she would have been raised and went on to raise two daughters in that same patriarchal world.

..

Doing the scientific testing and calculation necessary for a DNA test would be easier than understanding Section 6, which determines if one is eligible to claim Indigenous identity under the Indian Act. Though a DNA test is not required, a complicated formula for establishing percentage of Indigenous blood is involved.

..

My mother never finished high school, but she could add, subtract and calculate percentages in her head. I often wish I'd inherited that trait and others: the code for her dark eyes, her lithe brown body, that anger that hummed beneath her skin and propelled like an engine.

..

My great-grandmother Rosalie was born half W̱SÁNEĆ, half Scottish. She married a guy who was also half Salish, half Scottish. I can't establish whether he's from the Suquamish, Squamish or Tsleil-Waututh people, though he may have kinship ties with all three. According to the Indian Act, her parents' union made my grandmother Pearl a "half-breed," like her mother. That word *breed* is also used for cattle and dogs, and sometimes to denote a deliberate mixing of traits in order to create something else.

..

The precise quantity of my Indigenous blood would matter if I were to apply for status, which isn't status in the sense of owning a big house or having several letters behind your name. Howard Adler in his documentary on Indian status compares the numbers on the status card to the numbers tattooed on Jewish people during the Holocaust. Numbers that identify a people destined for removal.

..

My mother Rose was one-quarter, and that would make me one-eighth. Such is the formulation for blood quantum.

..

The DNA from ZIȻOT through Rosalie and Pearl, Rose, myself, and my daughter, whose middle name is Rose, shifted microscopically generation by generation. Imagine a time-lapsed film: skin whitening, the addition of freckles, my father's curly hair, until finally in my daughter's bright blue eyes our Indigenous blood is no longer perceptible.

# PLACE OF RUPTURE

## i) Afterglow

I'm looking for a linear path through my family history, but with so many fragments and silences to go on, I meet impasse. If I listen harder, might I resurrect the voices of the dead? It seems an act of mercy to at least imagine what it was like. This is the closest I can come to remembrance.

..

*In about 1891, a young Rosalie slogs up the hill from the harbour, the baby heavy on her chest, the putrid smoke from the kilns swirling around her; everything is soot smeared: brick, sky, the air. Though the muscles in her legs tremble and her heart drums beneath her lungs, her belly flutters with what she names happiness. When she reaches the top of the hill, she'll enter a short path through the woods to the little company house she shares with William and their daughter; two rooms and on the outside, whitewashed. She rushes so she'll make it home before the baby, breathing steadily now, awakens. Stella, her first-born.*

..

Stella was William and Rosalie Houston's oldest child, and my grandmother Pearl was their youngest. From what I can find, it seems two of their ten children didn't make it to adulthood. Until recently, I didn't know that after my grandmother's birth the family lived for three years on San Juan Island before they returned to Canada. The more I discover, the clearer it is that not knowing was a coping strategy my family used for two generations.

..

One day in the fall of 2019, an hour before sunset, my husband and I arrive on San Juan Island, and after dropping our bags at the B&B we hurry to Lime Kiln Park, me with notebook in hand and him with his camera. I'm there to mine my family history, my mother's side of the story, as if it's not something of me but outside of me.

We skirt an arbutus-clogged trail above the shore. At its end, a stone kiln from another century abuts the cliffside. There were nine such kilns on the island in the late nineteenth and early twentieth centuries, all of them burning limestone at 2,000 degrees F. Below where I stand on the edge of the quarry looms a heap of white marred rocks stilled in mid-landslide on the steep incline. When the quarry was in operation workers sometimes tumbled from that slope and drowned in Haro Strait, and the cold slap of the ocean for a brief few seconds must have been a welcome relief after the searing heat of the kiln.

..

My family history is slippery; if it were rock, it could slide so easily down a slope over other rocks and into the sea.

..

My mother didn't like her name, *Phyllis Stella Rose*—maybe because of the way my father popped each syllable from his mouth in a spray of pebbly "s" sounds, theatrical and mocking, and her children, including me, laughed with him, at her. Mocking. Now, five years since my mother's death, her name is the silence of a butterfly made audible. Said out loud it sputters with sibilance, flutters, takes flight then lands softly on a shortened version of my great-grandmother's name. She went by Rose.

..

My husband and I rush from the site of the kiln to make it back to the parking lot before dark. Small groups of people sit and stand along the shore in the enclosing dusk as if they're waiting for something. They peer across the water. I see nothing but the darkening sea where the sun is half-submerged and casts a creamy golden light onto the swollen stone above the water, turns the flesh of the arbutus a deep orange. A woman with binoculars dangling around her neck glances at us. "They're coming back," she says in a near whisper.

..

John S. McMillin was drawn to Roche Harbor by a ledge of limestone not far from Lime Kiln Park. He had an eye for a money-making natural resource, a talent for extraction. Limestone wedged along a ledge that extends above the shore over half a mile. When you read about McMillin, the word *visionary* is frequently invoked.

Google limestone pits if you know nothing about them, as I did, and you'll see photos of an eerie monochromatic world, thoroughly white under a blanket of limestone dust.

..

My great-grandparents—William and Rosalie Houston—were possibly drawn to San Juan Island not so much for the limestone ledge as the edge where they could be out of sight from a mainstream society that saw them as neither white nor Indigenous. According to an affidavit signed in 1914 by my great-auntie Laura, the Houston family were members of the "Mitchell Bay Indians," a self-identified assemblage of people from the Coast Salish tribes and nations living on San Juan Island, including the Lekwungen, Saanich, Lummi, Samish, Swinomish and Clallam. Laura's affidavit was one of several applications from Mitchell Bay Native Americans who didn't qualify for land allotments because their tribe wasn't officially recognized. Instead, they were applying for adoption into the Quinault Indian Nation who were, at the time, inviting in members of other tribes in an effort to retain their tribal land, as allotments of their lands would be made available to non-Natives if not claimed by Native Americans.

The 1887 General Allotment Act aimed at breaking up reservation land was an assimilationist policy.

It's hard to know what drove Laura to apply. On her application she states she "is desirous of a home of her own." She also declares that she is "married to a white man." Her application was rejected, as were many, for a number of reasons, including marriage with "non-American Indians." Meanwhile in Canada, First Nations women who married a white man lost their status, as would have been the case with both William and Rosalie's mothers.

To this day, the Mitchell Bay Band is one of several tribes who aren't recognized by the United States government. My great-grandparents, too, would have lived in this no man's land between Canadian citizenship and American citizenship, a Scottish ancestry and a Coast Salish ancestry. Between legitimacy and illegitimacy, a validated history and one considered invalid.

Back then San Juan Island had been caught in an identity crisis of its own, resolved only a few years before William and Rosalie married there in 1889. A long running cross-border dispute between the United States and Canada had ultimately been decided in favour of the United States in 1872, with the border between the two countries drawn down the middle of Haro Strait, thus severing Coast Salish territory. No matter that the island had been the home of the Songhees and the Lummi for thousands of years and a gathering place for many of the Coast Salish peoples from what are now Washington State and British Columbia.

..

I've come to associate my family history with lines of demarcation. Arbitrary borders for the sake of an uneasy peace, around which there is eruption and cover up.

..

I like to imagine that when she was a young girl Rosalie came across from W̱SÁNEĆ territory to San Juan Island in a canoe with her mother's people to gather camas bulbs, as generations of her people had done before her. It's possible they landed at K̲IK̲EL, the SENĆOŦEN word that means *lime* in English and identifies the place commonly known these days as Roche Harbor: *the place of lime*.

In 1889, the year my great-grandparents married, an article from the *Washington Standard* said that lime "in a state of purity is a white powder... so infusible as to resist a very intense heat."

Rosalie would have met William either on San Juan Island or across the strait in Saanich, BC. We know for a fact that they were married by a justice of the peace at the home of William's sister Emma and her husband on San Juan Island. On a document that came to me through the San Juan Island archives, signed by Emma, it states she belonged to the "Suquamish

Tribe of Indians" in Washington State near San Juan Island, which would mean so, too, did her brother William. A cousin once told me that the Houston side denied their Indigenous ancestry in a way the Bartleman side did not. This document would suggest otherwise, for Emma, at least. Other than that, I know little about William's history, though it would seem there were ties to the territory, not only on Rosalie's side but also on his. Fred, William's older brother named after my Scottish great-grandfather Alfred Houston, signed an affidavit that Rosalie and William were of marrying age. The marriage licence is dated "the 5th day of April, 1889." Let's say the sun shone and the fields were green and scattered with camas in blue bloom, the colour of the sky.

Did Rosalie miss her Saanich home, her SENĆOŦEN-speaking mother? Maybe, but they had their sights set on opportunity, a job, their beautiful young bodies drawn to one another: children.

In an old black and white photo from a book on local island history, the Roche Harbor Lime Works company houses are lined up in rows across a field of stumps, and the caption describes their setting as a "workman's utopia." I don't know if William, Rosalie and baby Stella lived in the employee cottages at Roche Harbor or even if William worked for McMillin, but it makes sense he was attracted to the employment possibilities with McMillin and that the cozy company cottages appealed to him and Rosalie, the prospect of steady work and the beauty of the island with its familial connections. I've seen records of my great-grandfather's employment at one or another kiln at different times.

..

Roche Harbor is no longer the hardscrabble company town it was when John S. McMillin ran the Tacoma and Roche Harbor Lime Company and my great-grandparents might have lived in the *workman's utopia*. Now Roche Harbor is considered a world-class resort, where the refurbished Hotel de Haro features the John Wayne suite with an extra-long tub, and in a faux-village atmosphere private Edwardian-style houses, condos and townhomes climb the hill from the harbour along green lawns and a path of interlocking brick and are rented out for sums far beyond William and Rosalie's imagination.

Outside McMillin's Dining Room expensive yachts and large cruiser boats line the slips at the marina, a shipshape blur of white under the overcast grey sky. The black Alaskan cod is rich and savoury with what the white-coated server described as a "racy" Sauvignon Blanc. My husband is talking about sailboats, pointing to one mast or the other, and I'm thinking of Rosalie, who is becoming something palpable as blood, my own. My gaze drifts from the marina toward the view above the harbour on the other side of the restaurant, where in my imagination expensive tourist accommodations dissolve into warehouses and rail lines, tall smokestacks, stumps along the hilltop and kilns.

..

*The field of stumps and the uniform little houses are in sight. Rosalie hurries because when Stella wakes, she'll wake like the wind on the sea from the north. Rosalie smiles to think of it. She wants a girl with gusto, a girl who'll accept no hand on her body except a loving one. Stella twists and moans in her sleep; who'd have thought that soft spot on a baby's head could smell so much like the tiny pink roses that bloom in the forest in early summer. If only her mother, her TÁN, could be here sniffing that sweetness. Oh, how Rosalie misses her; William promises they'll go in the summer to Saanich, bring her TÁN back to the island, if only she'll come.*

..

In the restaurant a man announces the colour ceremony. The servers in their white coats stand against the wall at attention with their hands folded in front of them. "O Canada" scrapes through the speakers and conversation at the tables around us is overtaken by the tuneless melody. The Canadian flag outside at the marina stairs, slack against its pole in the still evening air, drifts downward. Next, "God Save the Queen" and a limp British flag follow suit. I raise my eyebrows and grin at my husband. He looks quickly away. Brief cannon fire and "Taps" surges through the room. A pendulous American flag droops then drops slowly downward. A woman next to us with a string of pearls around her slender neck stares at her folded hands. It's hard to know what she's thinking. Her partner in a grey suit and tie has his eyes fixed on the flags. His barrel chest moves as if to match the rhythm of "The Stars and Stripes Forever." I catch my husband rolling his eyes, and I'm aware of chunks of dried mud falling off the sole of my hiking boots and slipping onto the floor beneath my feet. When it's clear it's all over, we grab for our Sauvignon Blanc. Presumably, behind the clouds the sun has dropped into the sea. We order the chocolate mousse.

..

You need only peruse the many black and white photographs of John McMillin, his swollen chest, chin tipped upward, wide lapel, spectacles, shaggy drooping moustache meant to look stylish, to know that he spent little time in the lime pits and to know he considered himself a man of stature, far above the men who moved mountains of lime rock for him so he might make his fortune. There's plenty of information about McMillin, including that he was an avid photographer, a republican and a member of a private, elitist club known to be attractive to men with business acumen, political aspirations and money: the Free Masons.

..

*"My daughter gets treated like fine china, that stuff the McMillins' got, same stuff I'm going to buy you one day," William says to Rosalie when he holds baby Stella on his lap so carefully, as if he's afraid she'll break, and Rosalie laughs. "She won't break, and I don't need no china," she says. He calls Stella his "little angel"—but never in his TÁN's language, only English from William's mouth. He says he can't be talking like an Indian on the job.*

..

The hellish heat, vertical slopes loose with stone underfoot, weight of rock, long hours, scrip, could explain why even if this were William's first job on the island, he didn't stay on in the *workman's utopia*. The *San Juan Islander* reports that he was employed over the years in a sandstone quarry, a lumber mill, chopping wood, farm work. And in 1895 William and his brother Fred made a land purchase at the head of Westcott Bay not far from Roche Harbor.

The day after our dinner at the resort, my husband and I drive along the road that skirts the narrow, sheltered Westcott Bay, past *Private, Keep Out* signs, past driveways that lead to luxury homes. The sun warms us through the car window. I imagine William and Rosalie somewhere in the vicinity in another time, a plough, a garden of vegetables, a horse and sheep. More babies: Fred, then Laura, Johnny, Ernie, then lastly my grandmother Pearl.

In 1903, at the age of six, Stella's little brother Johnny died from what was known as the "strangling angel of children." Diphtheria, a major cause of death at that time, primarily affected children. Johnny's neck would have been swollen into a "bull neck" while the house rattled with the clatter of the disease's characteristic barking cough, and the child's spasmodic, putrid breath clotted the air. The word *diphtheria* comes from the Greek word meaning leather, a simile for the pseudo-membrane that forms over the throat of the afflicted. The local paper reported that after Johnny's death the doctor visited the house to "establish a quarantine." And the house would have fallen silent.

..

My grandmother Pearl, said to be hardened against the past, in a gesture that suggests the opposite, gave my mother the name *Rose* after her mother and *Stella* after her sister. Did my grandmother share with my mother the story of her name's origin? Maybe my mother knew about Rosalie and about my great-auntie Stella and never told us—or she didn't know, or she told us and we all forgot. Such is my mother's history and therefore mine, full of not knowing and sort of knowing and much forgetting.

..

An antitoxin for diphtheria was developed in the 1890s, but it's impossible to know whether it was available on the island at the time of Johnny's illness. If it was, its cost was too dear for the Houstons, who didn't have the means of the current Westcott Bay dwellers.

The only remaining trace of Johnny consists of a few lines in the *San Juan Islander*, which noted the time and cause of death then went on to say:

> *The child was ill but a short time, the dread disease*
> *having attacked him in a most malignant form.*

Between these lines is the story untold: a family's grief, a mother who must be tough as leather.

..

When I told my father that my research confirmed my maternal grandmother's birth on San Juan Island, he said, "I always thought she was lying." When I added that Mom's grandfather once owned a thirty-acre ranch, my father, who's rarely speechless, had nothing to say.

..

*Rosalie closes the door of the little house behind her, glad to be out of sight of the nosy Mrs. Taylor. She continues with her daydreams. When William and his brother Fred buy a farm, she will learn how to grow potatoes, onions and carrots. Her TÁN never learned that, but Rosalie will. Like William always says, "Things are different now." Women don't have to go getting scratched up in the bush looking for berries when you can buy them with the scrip. Rosalie loves the ELILE best, how they brighten up the forest in summer's beginning like little sunrises hiding under the leaves, a tang on the tongue, and she'll pick them come June to mix with the salmon spawn if she can get some the way her TÁN did, her poor TÁN, so much is different now and so hard for her to learn new ways. Stella will be a help to Rosalie, like she was to her TÁN. How close she and this oldest daughter will be, her helpmate, someone she'll tell secrets to.*

..

Skinny-trunked firs close in on me and my husband, then we're in a scruffy open area known as the Roche Harbor Pioneer Cemetery. We're looking for Stella's grave—a cousin has told me it's somewhere on the island—and a clue as to the cause of her death. Picket fences painted white are scattered in enclosed squares big enough to contain a body or two, depending on the size. Inside a few of the fences are gravestones, though their inscriptions are indiscernible. The enclosures are overgrown with thistle and blackberry. I step carefully, sure that amidst the forest mulch there are other graves, unmarked and unfenced. If Stella is buried here, there's no possible way of knowing.

An inert sky hangs lowly, ready to rain. The air is saturated, and all the dead surround me and for a moment I lose track of who I'm looking for, surely not this great-auntie of whom I knew nothing months before. Yet I'm urged on by a need to confirm this ancestor's existence, to validate my mother's, my own, to link our history.

Finally defeated by the overgrowth and the scattered stone markers in the haphazard graveyard I follow my husband farther down the path. Minutes later, the spongy forest floor beneath our feet transitions into concrete and suddenly above the trees looms an ornate stone arch and we're in a clearing. We face an elegant stairwell that ascends to the middle of a circular temple. Seven Corinthian columns stretch upward. A round table of limestone surrounded by six stone and cement chairs sits in the middle of a temple. The whole structure is resplendent with Masonic and Methodist symbolism, down to the number of stairs. We are face to face with Afterglow, the McMillin family mausoleum.

The light is flat, and the mausoleum doesn't glow, though some say it does in a certain light. The temple before me is nothing more than a rupture on the landscape like a story gone awry or the sudden appearance of fenced-in yards for the unknown dead. The tiny graveyard a few metres away through the forest renders the edifice before us grotesque, a cruel absurdity.

..

On that first night on the island, my husband and I settle on the rocks not far from the woman with the binoculars. Across Haro Strait the sun has disappeared, leaving a hazy silhouette of Vancouver Island afloat while brushing the sky with colour in its wake: purple and pink, and inside a swirl of incandescent cloud at the horizon, a golden glow above Mt. Newton. The sea is shimmering now, and one dorsal fin then another slices its surface. Arching upward an orca appears, and another and another, then they plunge downward into the darkening sea and up again. We watch, weary from the day, and it seems there'll be no end. The whales continue to leap upward with the grace of arrows and enter the water again and again as if inspirited to do precisely what they've been doing for century after century. Across the strait on the Canadian side of the border Mt. Newton's rounded peak is lit in a soft blue light. ŁÁWELNEW is a sacred place to the W̱SÁNEĆ people. Tonight, an artificial line down the centre of the strait is of no consequence in the presence of the constant roar of the ocean and the whales leaping from its depths.

## ii) Pivot

I imagine it's 1904 and my fourteen-year-old great-aunt Stella is on the edge of a bear pit on legs thin as sticks beneath her school skirt. *She hunches her shoulders and holds her head slightly back as if steeling herself.*

*Bangs fringe her small face, and her wide dark eyes register not fear so much as recognition. She's transfixed, seeing something of herself in the bears' captivity, their restless pacing, and the way in which they stand on their hind legs sniffing the air, ever vigilant.*

On one of those West Coast mornings in early fall a mist hangs over the sea obscuring the view across the sound in front of our house. I've just returned from San Juan Island where I walked on the ground of my grandmother's birth and where her sister Stella had walked until she was sixteen years old. During my visit there, I'd failed to find Stella's grave or any information about her cause of death.

I sit at my desk, look over my notes, then after narrowing the search parameters I type *Stella Houston* into newspapers.com. An article from the *San Juan Islander* dated August 4, 1906, with the headline "Death of Stella Houston" fills my screen. *Stella Houston, eldest child of Mr. and Mrs. Wm. Houston, of Roche Harbor, died at the home of her parents, Wednesday, July 25, of consumption, aged 16 years, five months, and eleven days. A year or two ago Stella went to Chemawa, Oregon, and it was while there that she contracted the dread disease that terminated her life.*

I google *consumption* and discover its medical name is tuberculosis. I google *Chemawa* and discover it's the oldest continually operating Indian boarding school in the United States. I jump to other sites and read that four years before Stella would have attended Chemawa, 20,000 children were enrolled across the United States in a total of 408 American Indian boarding schools. I read that the schools deployed "systematic militarized and identity-alteration methodologies" in which "disruption to the family" was necessary to meet the goals of assimilationist policy.

I cannot read any more, so I sit for a long time watching the fog lift off the water. The sea has retreated and left in its wake the detritus of low tide, and it's as if I'm seeing it for the first time though the tide's rhythm, how it reveals and conceals, forms the backdrop of my days.

Chemawa, tuberculosis. This new information, always known on some level, I take as confirmation of my lineage, a lineage inseparable from this wound I've been excavating all along. Beneath the skin of my great-aunt and therefore my great-grandmother, my grandmother, my mother and myself, this wound has festered. My body trembles like a rattle, as if a shadow enters.

..

Once a massage therapist said to me after a treatment, "There's some old blockage." I told her about being hit by a car years before. She shook her head. "It goes further back than that, way back."

..

Was Stella's death the pivot in my family's ruptured history on which a choice about race turned? Was it the event that led to our claiming a white identity, to my coming to adulthood ignorant of my great-aunt's brief, tragic sixteen-year existence? How did my mother not know where her middle name came from? How could we not know Rosalie's Coast Salish mother was W̱SÁNEĆ, or whether William's Coast Salish mother was Suquamish or Tseil-Waututh? We know about the men—Peter Bartleman, who married Rosalie's mother, was a Scottish blacksmith and so, too, was Alfred Houston, who married William's mother—but we know little about the women.

Daniel Heath Justice, the Cherokee academic, speaking of what it means to be Indigenous, says, "rupture was our inheritance."

..

In his memoir, Edwin L. Chalcraft, who would have been the superintendent of Chemawa when Stella attended, described the school's bear pit as ten feet deep and twelve feet across. Its walls were steep without handhold or foothold, and we can assume escape was difficult, though not impossible.

Chalcraft doesn't identify the bears' species, nor does he allude to their huge paws or thick shiny coats. He doesn't mention how their skins once protected the people from the cold, and in return the people sang and drummed songs of gratitude. Despite having Arapaho students in his charge, he doesn't tell you the Arapaho story about how Trickster killed the children of the Bear Women. Instead, he calls them "pets" and names them Patsy and Annie. He says the bears amuse the students by performing tricks for peanuts and candy. And affecting a tone of playfulness, he goes on to claim that a yearly bit of fun the night before April Fool's Day was to release the bears from their pit to wander the grounds until noon the next day.

I imagine the bears' bid for freedom, how they might have scaled the edge of that chasm, hearts beating faster and blood flowing into their massive limbs, how they recalled the strength in their broad backs. And from the deep well of their memory did they draw the rhythm of the drums? On the three hundred acres belonging to the school where they found themselves, the two bears would have bounded across the farm by way of the dairy buildings under the ornamental trees and shrubs and slipped past the rose bushes along the cement walkways toward the massive brick dorms where the children slept.

..

Superintendent Chalcraft proudly titled his memoir *Assimilation's Agent*. He was a professional colleague and admirer of General Richard Pratt, a man credited with the creation of industrial complex–sized, paramilitary, off-reservation Indian boarding schools. In 1892, Pratt famously said, "Kill the Indian in him, and save the man," and it was this doctrine which guided Chalcraft in managing the school.

Did my two Coast Salish great-grandmothers make the choice between Indigenous and settler when they married white men around 1866, or was it ten years later when the first Indian Act officially removed their Indian status because of these marriages? Did the rupture occur with one of the many revisions to the act—the one that empowered the Indian agent to remove persons from the reserve?

Perhaps the line was drawn, the binary between white and Indian established, when Rosalie's mother's people were forced onto reserves or when the first residential schools were opened. Or when Rosalie moved away from her mother and the Saanich people, or when William learned if he wrote *Scottish* by the question of ancestry on official forms, he'd more easily acquire employment and government services. It could be the line was drawn when six-year-old Johnny died from diphtheria in 1903 and a year later William was seriously injured, and shortly afterwards Stella and Fred, her younger brother, were sent to Chemawa, over three hundred miles away from home.

..

*Stella tucks the violin under her chin and raises the bow the way Mr. Turney showed them; its heft presses on her shoulder and an edge digs into her collar bone. Her instrument is so heavy today, in this room with its overstuffed couches and dark furniture, plates bulging with fruit and sandwiches on the sideboard.*

*Her stomach is knotted and her forehead bubbles with sweat, but Stella can't take her eyes off those mountains of food. She's all bone today, no muscle. Small windows high on the walls discharge a dim light, yet it's as if the sun is beating on her and this grand house is made of glass, like the hothouses at school where they grow the tomatoes. White women, their hair piled high under hats that threaten to topple them over, and men in ties and vests, sit in the rows of chairs staring like they've never seen an Indian band before.*

*The white woman in the beaded doeskin dress who lives in this house with her husband, the judge, smiles at Stella—at least she wants that smile to be meant for her, that white woman's smile—and at the same time Stella recoils, fills with shame for the sweat under her armpits, the weakness all over her stinking body, her jet-black hair with its chopped bangs.*

*Her violin squeals, and Margaret, who plays beautifully—Margaret who always plays beautifully according to Mr. Turney—giggles beside her. She loves Margaret, who is Tlingit from Alaska, and someday Stella will go with her to see the midnight sun. But now she wants to put her in a headlock like she did when Margaret snuck cigarettes into their dorm room. "You asking for a beating?" Stella had said. "I'll give you one."*

*All the white people are clapping now and Mr. Chalcraft steps forward. He wiggles his moustache the way he does before he speaks, and Margaret giggles again. This time her giggle fills the quiet room, and when Mr. Chalcraft pauses and looks toward the girls, Stella's stomach clenches. The heat washes over her body, and her chest tightens. She's afraid she's going to cough. The woman in the doeskin dress thanks Mr. Chalcraft for coming and thanks Mr. Turney who bows.*

*On the way to the reception, Stella heard Mr. Chalcraft explain that the woman is "a great patron of the Indian arts." "As am I," he added. Later, Margaret will whisper that Mr. Chalcraft wanted to make love to the white woman in the doeskin dress.*

*On every wall of the room woven cedar baskets, even more magnificent than what Stella's grandmother makes, are on display behind glass doors.*

*"You can see for yourself" says Mr. Chalcraft, "the Indian is as capable of high attainment in arts as his paler brother." He puffs up his chest and hooks a thumb in each lapel of his jacket.*

*Then Mr. Turney starts talking about Mozart again, and the room begins to spin. Stella tries to focus on a ledge nearby where red and yellow dahlias spill from a brass bowl. Margaret motions for her to hoist her violin, and Stella sees that she's leaning as if the weight of the instrument is pulling her toward the floor. She'll refuse to go to the infirmary when she gets back to the school. She and Fred will run away. Anyone who goes to the infirmary disappears.*

*She lifts the violin, but her arms are wobbly and weak. White faces stare and stare. Everyone is clapping. Stella's never seen a house this grand, that much food except when her Dad brought home deer meat, and sometimes in the summer all the berries, and the garden. She won't think about home, and she won't go to the infirmary. The room spins in a whirl of faces and voices. She would rather weave baskets with her grandmother than play the violin. Sweat slimes her face, and she realizes she's dangling her instrument. Mr. Chalcraft strides toward her through the crowd. The violin slides from her hand and lands on the floor with a clunk.*

*"What is the matter with you, girl?"*

*Stella can't find any words, not English, not SENĆOŦEN. It's as if the words are stuck deep inside her and will remain there for a long time.*

..

Chalcraft, in his biography, quotes a Seattle magazine from 1909 that describes a music reception at the home of Judge and Thomas Burke much like that imagined above. In fact, Stella died before this reception, and wouldn't have been there. But such a scene captures the attitudes that prevailed in the school that she attended only long enough to contract a deadly disease. With so little known about my great-aunt, all I can do is place her in the culture that contributed to her early death. Dahlia-filled brass bowls, a detail in the article, complete the chilling burlesque quality, the affectation toward a brutal gentility; children turned artifact.

..

The few facts I can find suggest that Fred and Stella were spared the fate of so many Native American and First Nations children in that they weren't forcibly removed from their home and sent to an Indian school. However, to what degree did coercion, assimilationist attitudes, and/or dire circumstances play a role in their attendance at Chemawa, located near Salem, Oregon, some twelve or more hours by ferry and train from their home on San Juan Island?

..

*When the doctor's wagon rolled up the road to the house, Rosalie was standing at the sink wringing her hand, scared it was carrying the corpse of her husband. Fred was with his dad and helped the doctor carry him into the house.*

*William was swathed in bandages across his chest and wheezing, but he managed a smile for her, even a joke. "And not even a deer to show for it," he said. She smiled back and squeezed his hand tight, knew it wasn't the time to ask about how they were supposed to get through Christmas in three weeks' time, let alone how they were going to manage the rest of their lives. Not the time to tell him she saw it coming with that Johnson, his hunting partner. Everyone knew Johnson liked his beer too much and got it from a guy in Friday Harbor who'd sell to Indians. Her William would never mistake a man for a deer like that fool did.*

*The newspaper fellow came around and there was an article in there, so everyone on the island knew their business. But people helped, especially those from Mitchell Bay.*

*The bullet went into him on the left side just below the collarbone and came out under the right collarbone clean through the lungs. William was going to have to pull breath in through one bullet hole and expel it through the other. He was going to have to breathe through his wound.*

*It didn't take him down, and it made Rosalie almost forget about Johnny, their little boy who'd died only months earlier from diphtheria. They had kids to raise, she and William. They weren't done yet, and they would figure it out.*

..

I've seen my mother steel herself against the day, my father's fresh wreckage our dawn, me and my silent siblings scrubbing for school, my mother for her meat-wrapping job at Woodward's. My father either absent or hang-dog, absent either way.

I've felt the grip of my mother's fingertips in my shoulders, even now can hear her hissed "Don't slouch." Never, no matter what. Don't slouch.

..

When I recently explained the seasons to my fair-skinned, blue-eyed four-year-old grandsons I found my hand sweeping around an imaginary circle in midair, and it's this circumvolution that makes me think there was no defining moment that marked the whiteness that is my family history. Long after Chemawa, my grandmother, Stella's sister, denied she had First Nations heritage. Years later my mother died without knowing her history. It is a narrative that is not linear, doesn't have a beginning, middle and end, because the questions are still being asked, the looking back over the shoulder then forward to the grandchildren, to the ruptures in a life.

### iii) Epistolary: File #2395

In late fall of 2019, several weeks after my return from San Juan Island, I receive an email from the Seattle Archives. It begins with an apology and an explanation that all they've found of Stella's Chemawa school file is the number 2395. It goes on to say that the *contents are missing, possibly removed. You could contact the school. It's still in operation.* Two emails to Chemawa, and a year later, I continue to wait for a reply. I am soon to learn that this is not unlike my great-grandparents' efforts at communication with Chemawa School over a hundred years before.

The archives, however, have attached Stella's brother Fred Houston's file. It contains image after image of letters dated between July 1906 and August 1907, most on yellowed stenographer's paper and addressed to *Mr. Chalcraft.* I pause to peruse one. The handwriting is tidy and legible with flourishes on the tails of the letter y and curlicues on the letter h, a weightlessness to it as if the writer's been careful not to press too hard with the pen. It's signed *Mrs. William Houston.* I read the signature again and again, as I slowly grasp in whose hand it's been written. This is the closest I've ever been to my great-grandmother Rosalie.

I scroll through the letters and discover some written by my great-grandfather, William Houston, as well as others from a family friend. There is one from the local doctor. These letters are regarding Fred, but they reveal Stella's story. I stare at the window, but because it's night my own murky reflection glances off a shiny black surface. It's hard, it's hard to read these letters and not feel immobilized. How can I write about this? In what way can I even think about it? I sit in silence.

I've included excerpts from several of the letters transposed exactly as they appear on the digital images including spelling and punctuation errors.

The letters that are from my own imagination are in italics, including those I've imagined from myself and from Stella.

**July 3, 1906**
Mr. Chalcraft, Sir
Will you grant Mr. Houston a favor by sending his son Fred come home? His Daughter Stella is very low. He will send money as soon as we hear from you.

Yours Truly,
C. O. French [a family friend whose sons attend Chemawa with Fred]

**July 14, 1906**
Mr. Chalcraft, Dear Sir
Stella is very sick so low she is in bed has to be helped, an is failing right along she is always speaking of her brother Fred would like to see him so we would like very well to get him home for her sake an please let us know what the fair is an we will send the money. The French boy is coming home send him with they. Please answer.

Yours Truly,
Mrs. William Houston

..

*July 25, 1906*
*Dear Mr. Chalcraft,*

*Here's what it means... to be failing right along at the end of consumption, so weak that you don't want to get up, sip on soup for your mother's sake to make her believe you're getting better when you know you're not. It means to be swallowed whole, the cough like a creature inside you that wishes to shatter your bones and make you bleed. You know this is what your mother has seen before, the lungs of her child hacking at the air starved for breath, with your little brother Johnny, his neck swollen into a bull neck. His was a contagion of another kind. Don't make her see it again, you tell yourself.*

*   And the cold that vice-grips every muscle, your mother wraps you in her shawl and for a moment you're warmed with her smell and the shawl's rough weave until the heat becomes a hot coal at your core radiating outward and your body thrashes against its wrapping and your mother's hand wound with cool cloth comes to your forehead.*

*   The nurse at the school didn't know your name. She called you nothing. Your mother's crinkled brow, her downturned mouth. You want her*

*to laugh that big laugh, to pull you on to her lap and at the same time you want her to go away so you don't infect her with your vile sickness. She mops up the blood that spews from your mouth when you cough. Your brothers and sisters hover at the door. "Go," you want to scream, "I have nothing for you but disease."*

*Your father takes orders from your mother, hoists you onto the bedpan, brings fresh water. He sags in the chair beside your bed, his hand limp in yours, but won't look you in the eye as if it's him who sickened you, or is it that he's sickened by you. You can't stand his helplessness; his shame sickens you. His shame now your shame.*

*When you could still stand, in the morning you left the hospital and attended your morning classes, and in the afternoon went either to the fields or the sewing room. You washed in the same trough as the other students, ate the same vile food in the dining room, worked alongside them.*

*The school hospital stunk of piss and blood, beds lined up so close, and the little ones sharing a bed. You heard the nurse say there were close to two hundred children in there all at once just after Christmas. You shivered under the one thin blanket and longed for the fever to crawl across your body. The coughing all night long and the crying for their mamas, your body's strength depleting.*

*The school sent you home before you became their statistic. In years to come they'll remove the contents of your file and send the contents of your brother Fred's file to the national archives. They won't answer your great-niece's emails the same way they didn't answer those letters from your mother and father.*

*You call again for Fred, your younger brother, twelve years old, who cried every day when you first went to the school. How you told him to shut up, slapped him once and said, "Better me than them." Has the creature entered your brother's lungs, pillaged his muscles? "Fred," you try to scream, but words shrivel at your lips.*

*Fred cannot stay there. At that school. Send him home.*

*The reek of the school's infirmary clings to your skin, and the memory of that girl in the next bed, not her but her body, shrouded in a white sheet: so still all the hours of the night until they took her away in the morning.*

*"Make him come home," you repeat over and over to your mother, your voice a whimper. If you could scream, you would, but it would shred what's left of your lungs.*

*Yours Truly,*
*Stella Houston*

**July 21, 1906**
Dear Mr. Chalcraft, Sir,

I enclose $12 for Freddy Houston fare. Pls send him soon as you can for Stella is failing fast and drop me a line. State what day Freddy leaves the school so I can have my sister in Seattle look out for him at the staishon and she can put him on the boat to come home.

From
William Houston

*July 25, 2021*
*Dear Great Auntie Stella,*

*What does it mean to "fail right along" while longing to see your younger brother? Not just for the way he makes you laugh, shares your memories, but to keep him safe the way you were supposed to. I had a younger brother and I could do nothing to keep him safe from dying. The difference is Fred survived, and you didn't, my dear Auntie.*

*When, after many years in Toronto, my brother returned here to the West Coast, he stayed alone at what was our summer cabin for a while because he had nowhere to live. He called me every day at my house one hundred kilometres away. He wanted me to come. I heard the anger in his voice.*

*"On the weekend, maybe not this one, the following weekend," I said.*

*My brother didn't say he was dying, but the signs were there. I knew how sick he'd been. There was no time: my children, the job.*

*Fred was only a child and the school wouldn't have told him anything. Your parents tried to get him home. If he'd known, he would have run. He did run, you know, but it was too late. When I finally made it to the Seattle Archives, I saw his name in the runaway book, scratched there along with all the others. He ran twice in February 1907. That's all it says, that he ran, not why or where or what happened to him when he was caught. He'd had enough by then, I suppose, and maybe only learned of your death through other students coming to the school.*

*Your great-niece,*
*Judy*

**Aug 11, 1906**
Dear Mr Chalcraft, Sir

I will ask you again to pleas send my son Freddy Houston Home for I have wrote two letters to you asking for freddy to come home and you said he should come and his fair money is there and if you would Be so kind and send him home it would cheer our home for we are feeling very sad over the loss of our daughter Stella Houston

Yours truly
William Houston

**Aug. 11, 1906**
Fred Houston

My Dear Boy I will write you a few lines to let you know that we send $12 to the Supertender Mr Chalcraft last month it was on the 19th of July, we received the return card on the 27th of July, we been expecting you home everyday the reason I never wrote to you any sooner. You speak to the supertender Mr Chalcraft. If he is not there hand it to Mr Cambell. If the French boy is coming home you come with them. If they are not comming home you come anyhow. We wrote two letters to the supertender Mr. Chalcraft to send you home last month well this is all hoping to see you soon.

From your Dear Mother
Mrs. Wm. Houston
I cannot tell you more will wait until you come home

..

*July 25, 2021*
*Dear Auntie Stella,*

*I sat by my brother's hospital bed in the last week of his life and watched his body's incremental shut down. It may be merciful that Fred wasn't there to watch yours do the same, but that's not true. It was a privilege to be with my brother. I wish so much for you that Fred could have been there.*

*In his last hours, the nurse showed me how to swab my brother's lips with moisture. "It's okay," she said, "You won't get it."*

*At first I thought she meant death, and I wanted to argue with her. None of us are spared. But no, she meant HIV, another contagious virus, and I said, "I know."*

*How could she think I didn't know? My brother had been HIV-positive for twenty years.*

*I took the Q-tip between my fingers, dabbed it in water and touched it to his parched lips. I told him I was sorry for everything I ever did that hurt him. I felt my shame. I feel shame when I think of you, Auntie, dying in the way you did.*

*Your great-niece,*
*Judy*

..

**Nov. 10, 1906**
Mr. Chalcraft, dear sir

I will drop this few lines to you about the money that I had sent for Freddy fair to come home.
you can put it in the Bank
And let him share what he wants at anytime
How is freddy is he well
Please see that Freddy has care about his neck
We was told that it was getting worse and see that he goes to the doctor
From William Houston

As much I've been attempting to shatter the constraints of time and place between myself and my ancestors, it's necessary to account for both to understand the meaning behind these letters. Calculate, as William and Rosalie would have painstakingly done, the dates of each letter factored against the length of time it should have taken for them to travel through the mail to Chalcraft's desk three hundred miles away, and when they might reasonably have expected a reply. Every second lengthening into moments then into taut hours while Stella's breath quickened toward the complete silence following her last. And that silence must have been clogged with the absence of word from Chemawa.

..

**March 16, 1907**
Mr Chalcraft, Dear Sir

Just a few lines to ask you about My son. Fred. I have not heard from him since January I am so uneasy about him please let us know how he is right away. I worry so about him afraid he is sick.
from Mrs Wm Houston

..

*July 25, 2021*
*Dear Auntie Stella,*

*After he learned he was HIV positive, whenever my brother flew to the coast for a visit, we walked around his diagnosis as if it were a black hole in the middle of the kitchen floor. We were a family practised at vigilance.*

*Novelist Eden Robinson says, "Black holes haunt your heaven. They warp space, bend time..."*

*My brother died in 2006 in the month of May. You died one hundred years earlier in the month of July. My mother cried for a long time, as I'm sure your mother did. I only hope she forgave herself for sending you to that school. She was told so many lies. She would have felt powerless—as did my mother, as did I.*

*I have this false idea I could have spared my little brother, not his life—that was out of my hands—but some of his pain. I guess my mother felt that way too, but we didn't talk about it much before she died.*
*Without knowing your physical suffering nor the wound inflicted by that boarding school, this is as close as I can come to begin to feel as you might have felt. That yearning, that shame.*

*Your great-niece,*
 *Judy*

..

**July 12, 1907**
Mr Chalcraft
Dear Sir

I am going to write a few lines asking you when you can send my boy Fred, home, I would be so pleased to hear from you please write an let me know... for I am going as far as Seattle to meet him. I would go to Chemawa an meet him an to visit the school to, but you see we have not got the money to spare for my husband is sick part of the time he cannot work so that makes money so scarce with us, if you can please let me know when you can send Fred home I would be the happiest woman living, I have never had a happy day since we lost our Dear girl Stella an that's a year ago this month...It will lighten my heart to see him once more...
Mrs. Wm Houston

DEPARTMENT OF THE INTERIOR
UNITED STATES INDIAN SERVICE

U.S. Indian Training School
Chemawa, Ore. July 17, 1907

Mrs. Wm Houston,
Roche Harbor, San Juan, Wash.,

Dear Madam:
I have your letter of the 12th, relative to Fred spending his vacation with
you this summer. In reply, I would say that Fred has been here during his
period of enrollment, three years and I can send him to you after school
closes. The Commencement will be at the end of the month and you may
look for Fred shortly afterwards. I will inform you and make arrangements
for your meeting him, as you suggested in your letter.

Very respectfully,

Superintendent.

..

*July 25, 2021*
*Dear Mr. Chalcraft,*

*You were a practised bureaucrat, disciplined, good with details. I'll give
you that. You unfailingly adhered to policy, then in 1910 something went
wrong, didn't it. Something snapped. The physical exertion that it must
have taken you to switch the backs and shoulders of those thirteen girls.
Did you admonish them while you did it, did you call them whores and
accuse them of sneaking off to meet their boyfriends? Your school was
being criticized for "immorality" around that time. Some girls got pregnant. When you were beating those girls, did they call for their mothers?
Did you know any of their names? You must have been out of breath by
the end of it all. Their offence was going for an evening walk without
supervision.*

*The good bureaucrat you were should have known that corporal
punishment had been banned by then. Not that it didn't go on, of course,
but you must admit, it was unbecoming behaviour from a top administrator such as yourself. Maybe if you hadn't ordered the older girls to whip
the others until they cried, which finally resulted in broken bleeding skin.*

*Maybe if you hadn't shouted at them to leave then, you didn't care, and three of them ran away that very night, maybe if you hadn't done that, you might not have been dismissed. It's not that you didn't manage to get yourself reinstated in the Indian Service before the year was out. It wasn't the first time for you, was it? It's true that your administration was riddled with incompetence, infighting and petty competition, and your argument that there were those who wanted your position might have been valid, but what saved you was your fierce defence of obedience at all costs and resolute belief in the goals of assimilation. What I'd like to know is if you ever feared that the massive social experiment in which you were a mere cog was at best a complete failure, and at worst a grotesque example of cultural genocide. Did you ever have doubts, Chalcraft, did it ever unsettle you that you had blood on your hands?*

*You and your kind came like predators for the children; you cut out the tongue so there would be no language, lopped off the legs so there would be no dance, no story, no song. You starved the belly of the nourishment that had sustained for thousands of years, so that the children became ill, and many died.*

*Like a matryoshka doll, my great-auntie Stella's brief, pillaged life nests inside the history of a family, which nests within the history of those nations born out of the brutal aggressions of colonialism. The truth is, Chalcraft, assimilation failed. If you didn't kill your protégés, as you did my great-auntie, you cast them into a troubled, fractured identity in which they wrestled with shame and a sense of a lost home. Perhaps Stella's youth and only brief exposure to your school spared her the self-loathing and denial passed through my grandmother and my mother to land on myself. You and your kind would fraction me up, champion the whiteness forced on me when from grief too hard to bear the mothers in my line disavowed Stella's short life, then went on to rewrite their histories in white marriages.*

*The irony is that those who've survived have learned to use your weapon—an education in the white man's ways—in the act of resistance. The survivors have learned to articulate their histories in a language their oppressors understand and to hold the truth before them as if they held up a mirror. We live in a time of reckoning. Your legacy is being called to account, Chalcraft. There'll be no resting in peace for you.*

*Sincerely,*
*Judy LeBlanc, great-niece of Stella Houston*

*July 25, 2021*
*Dear Auntie Stella,*

*One hundred and fifteen years ago today, you died.*

*This morning on the spreading clear-cut where I walk my dog, the black seed pods of the invasive Scotch broom rattled in the hot dry air. We've been thirty-nine days without rain and there's no end of this drought in sight, a record in this temperate rainforest that is the traditional territory of the Coast Salish people. A few weeks ago, in one of the province's many ravaging wildfires, the town of Lytton burned to the ground, leaving its residents, many from Lytton First Nation, homeless. And at the beginning of the summer 182 graves were discovered on the site of a former Indian residential school in Kamloops, BC, which triggered discoveries at other residential school sites across Canada, as well as a commitment from US Interior Secretary Deborah Haaland, a Laguna Pueblo woman, to investigate unmarked gravesites at American Indian boarding schools, both former and present. High on her list is Chemawa, the oldest continuously operating school of its kind.*

*This past Canada Day I hung an orange shirt at the start of my driveway. People are doing this to bring attention to the children buried in unmarked graves at the residential school sites, and there was a movement to forego Canada Day celebrations in their memory. I hid in the house away from the fire engines circling the neighbourhood and blasting their horns, Canadian flags snapping from their flanks. Some mistook it for a fire. I thought of you and Fred.*

*I walk on the shore near where I live and I'm comforted by the everchanging blue face of the sea, where my brother's ashes were spread. Though I've searched, I can't find where you are buried, but Google took me to information on your brother Fred, including the whereabouts of his gravesite. He came to Canada with your parents a few years after you died, after my grandmother was born, and he went on to serve in the First World War. I still don't know where my grandmother—your youngest sister, whom you never met—went to school. She gave my mother your name, so it seems you've never been forgotten. I like to think maybe you were a bit like my mother.*

*It's nothing to hang an orange shirt in a driveway, a mere gesture really.*

*In a few years I'll be approaching old age. It's taken this long, but once there's a knowing there can be no unknowing. Much has been underground for too long: the remains of children long grieved, the histories untold.*

*Sincerely,*
*Your great-niece Judy LeBlanc, great-granddaughter of Rosalie Houston (née Bartleman), granddaughter of Pearl Van Horlick (née Houston), daughter of Stella Rose LeBlanc (née Van Horlick)*

# WALKING IN THE WOUND

The blurred outline of a lone fisherman emerges out of the morning fog along the shore. It's October 2021, and we're well into the fourth wave of the COVID-19 pandemic. I sit at my desk and through the window I watch the fisherman cast and cast again. I've spent the morning digging on the web, which has led me to the report now open on my computer screen. From the Tŝilhqot'in Nation, it's titled *Dada Nentsen Gha Yatastig*; in English this means *I am going to tell you about a very bad disease.*

..

English ivy creeps from the neighbour's yard and embeds its tiny rootlets into the fence, concealing the boards behind a leafy curtain. We tear at it, but it persists. It's the same with the field bindweed that spreads even faster, draping the bank along the shore and twining around the barbed leaves of the native mahonia and the Nootka rose. A lover of disturbed sites, it occupies the space beneath and around the stairs to the beach below our house. Its leaves are the shape of arrowheads, and its vine—skinny as thread—is easy enough to snap with a flick of the thumbnail, but the roots crawl underground, where they trace great networks impossible to dislodge. In this way, they record a history on the land.

..

Disease, too, writes a history. My great-aunt Stella was one of many children—roughly one in five at the time—who returned home from a Native American boarding school with tuberculosis, or TB, only to die shortly afterwards. TB, a bacterial infection primarily affecting the lungs, spread in Native American boarding schools during the last half of the nineteenth and the first half of the twentieth century. The situation in Canada wasn't any better. Canada's first chief officer of medical health, Dr. Peter Bryce, states in his report from 1907 that tuberculosis was rampant in Indigenous residential schools, with 24 percent of students dying either at school or soon after leaving. David Dejong, author and Indigenous studies scholar, refers to TB as the "scourge" of Indian country.

..

When I attempt to sketch a family tree, names and dates multiply, burgeon outward and lengthen into branches that cross over one another, leaving gaps and blank spaces. This family tree, as if it were a live thing, fans into a filigree in which patterns repeat, then abruptly end, then start up again. A creeping rootstock.

..

The Tŝilhqot'in Nation report, dated March 2021, is about a twenty-first-century scourge. A pull quote in the introduction reads: *This report is specific to the COVID-19 pandemic. But the message that emerges is that the emergency is not simply the pandemic. Rather, the underlying and ongoing emergency is the persistence of colonialism in Canada.*

..

Some days all I see are invasive species. I walk the dog at the base of the mountain on old logging roads overgrown with Himalayan blackberry, bracken, various thistles and columns of Scotch broom. In 1850, Captain Walter Grant, a Scottish settler, brought Scotch broom back from Hawaii and planted it on his Sooke farm. Perhaps he was attracted by the prospect of hillsides lit up in springtime with the shrub's bright yellow flowers. As it turns out, these flowers are toxic to humans and animals, and broom displaces native and beneficial plants. The problem is so bad on Vancouver Island that a volunteer group named Broombusters sets out every spring to clear roadsides, parks and properties of the infestation.

..

Up until the 1950s, the "virgin soil" theory, which held that Indigenous people hadn't been exposed to the diseases of the white man, and therefore were more susceptible to illness, was the most widely accepted explanation for the higher rates of TB amongst the Indigenous population. This belief persisted despite mounting research implicating socio-economic conditions and evidence confirming the presence of TB antibodies and long-healed lesions in Indigenous people. In a 2021 CBC article titled "Why have Indigenous communities been hit harder by the pandemic than the population at large?" Ainsley Hawthorn claims that the virgin soil theory absolved European settlers of "any moral responsibility for depopulation."

What responsibility do we have toward one another? According to Indigenous Services, as of December 2021 there were twice as many active cases of COVID-19 on First Nations reserves than in the general Canadian population. The Tŝilhqot'in report outlines disparities in access to clean drinking water and health services between Indigenous and settler communities. Food insecurity, underemployment, poverty and insufficient data tracking the numbers and locations of infections increase the risk of contracting COVID-19. These conditions exist in First Nations communities across Canada as well as across Native American communities, making them *vulnerable*, not *susceptible*, to higher incidences of disease.

..

In 1870, a doctor who worked with the Winnebagoes said, "The prevailing disease is tuberculosis, which is slowly, but surely, solving the Indian problem."

..

The dog and I walk on the deserted logging road, and above us clear-cuts dot the mountainside like raw sores and the power line snakes upward until it disappears. Its transmission towers and cables link one to another, scoring an avenue through the forest and across the mountainsides in all directions. In the distance, the Island Highway hums with traffic heading north and south or to one of three ferry terminals where cars cross the water to meet the network of roads that trace an entire continent.

..

Great Aunt Stella was of mixed race, and her Indigenous ancestors had lived amongst white settlers and been exposed to their diseases for over a century. She contracted TB at age fourteen in 1905 while attending Chemawa Indian Boarding School near Salem, Oregon, with around six hundred other students. A document from the Seattle Archives lists 148 children in the school hospital when Great Aunt Stella was admitted in January 1905, roughly 25 percent of the school's population. The Meriam Report released in 1928 delivered a scathing assessment of the conditions in Native American boarding schools. Poor nutrition, overcrowded dormitories, and unsanitary living conditions were ideal conditions for the spread of disease. My great-grandparents were not told that their daughter Stella was ill with tuberculosis until just before the school sent her home to die.

..

The 2021 Tŝilhqot'in report states it is "racism, not race, that is a risk factor for dying of COVID-19."

..

Near the gravel pit off the logging road, a handful of bullet shells are scattered on the ground, along with squished beer cans. A pie plate nailed to a tree shows evidence of target practice. I'm grateful there's no one around today. Gun blasts put me on edge—so too the thought of a cougar somewhere in the trees, waiting. But this is my familiar state, the body never quite relaxed. I'm at home with the scruff and scramble, the struggle between old mountains, cedar and shifting sky—and a rude and invasive species. My ear attuned for guns and cougars, for signs of ruin.

..

When my dog and I walk alone on the mountain, I carry a stick carved from a laurel branch, another invasive that we've been unable to eradicate from our yard but do keep under control. The stick is of a dense, heavy wood that might one day protect me from a cougar. I don't know if there's a cougar nearby, but there's always the possibility: Vancouver Island has the highest concentration of them in North America.

Hypervigilance is considered a symptom of trauma. I think of family stories not told, my mother's mistrust of others, how my father said she was "slow to warm." I recall her quick intake of breath, widened eyes, the tension in her jaw at the first sign of trouble: an overlooked bill, a busy highway, a sick grandchild.

..

At the beginning of the first wave of the COVID-19 pandemic, a Yellow-head Institute researcher, Courtney Skye from the Six Nations, said on CBC that withholding data about specific whereabouts of COVID-19 cases undermines Indigenous autonomy and puts Indigenous lives at risk. Know-ing there exists a threat in one's environment without having any specific information or agency to act on it engenders what Skye calls a "vigilante mentality."

..

Sometimes I long for a freckle-less skin, my mother's smooth brown limbs. I feel—what is it?—shame that I pass so much more easily than she did, that she and I knew so little about our Coast Salish ancestry, that we knew nothing about Auntie Stella. I have a house on the beach on the traditional territory of the Pentlatch-speaking people, whose numbers were signifi-cantly reduced by two smallpox epidemics, war with the Ligwiłda'xw peo-ple from the north and encroachment from settlers. Their children would have been sent to residential schools. This I've only learned recently, and the more I learn, the more it's as if the past merges with the present. I live in a high-ceilinged waterfront house on land that thrums with history. Sometimes my privilege feels like a sentence, the cost of my grandmother's betrayal of her ancestry, my family's denial.

..

I write a brief article for the Fanny Bay flyer, an appeal to organize the community to rid the beach of its bindweed. I describe the proliferation of this invasive species on the bank and the potential destruction to the coastal vegetation above the shore. No one contacts me.

..

Knowledge doesn't lead to change, though wisdom may. A strong sense of equity forms the foundation of wisdom and at its base lies a recognition of the interconnectedness of all living things, or *interbeing*, a term coined by the Buddhist teacher Thich Nhat Hanh. This echoes the expression "all my relations," used amongst many Indigenous communities to reflect a worldview that acknowledges an interdependence between all that exists in the universe. The shore is me and you are me. I am you. So, too, the native kinnikinnick and mahonia. We keep one another in balance: you, me and the mahonia, and therefore we are responsible for one another.

..

I want to know, but not in the way one knows after reading books on racism and attending talks on cultural sensitivity. I want to walk through a clear-cut and let the distant squeal of a saw and the echoing scream of a cougar fracture the silence; I want to yank and twist the Scotch broom away from the kinnikinnick so hard I get blisters on my hands, maybe even blood—to feel hopelessness, but I won't stop. I think what I mean is I want to know it in the body, to sit for uncomfortable hours and meditate on loss.

..

Although the term *soul wound* has been expropriated by pop culture, according to Native American psychologist Eduardo Duran, it has long been an integral part of Indigenous knowledge and used to describe the multigenerational debilitating distress that is the result of colonization. In the *International Handbook of Multigenerational Legacies of Trauma*, Duran et al. describe the symptoms of *acculturative stress* as "anxiety, depression, feelings of marginality and alienation, heightened psychosomatic symptoms, and identity confusion."

My mother telling me months before she died that she didn't know where she belonged. And years before, when my father called to say she'd fallen, that it was hardly a fall but she wouldn't get up and she wouldn't let him near. He put her on the phone.

"He says there's no pain, it's all in my imagination."

There was pain.

..

A clear-cut is a wound on the landscape. From the highway, these logged patches make the mountain appear scraped raw, and as you drive north on Vancouver Island past smaller and increasingly remote communities, the clear-cuts spread wider and are more frequent. The heavily populated south Island was logged, subdivided and developed nearly two centuries ago. At its tip in Victoria, where I lived for most of my life, it was easy to forget. Unlike in the Comox Valley, I wasn't confronted daily with the remains of a greener day, an immense forest from a time that is slipping away. I guess I was insulated from the past, but now I think I was missing something. When I walk in the wound on the mountain, I'm surrounded by life struggling to carry on. Awareness of this struggle comes more from a deep knowing than from seeing, does not come easily, but is a result of seeking.

The dog and I know places on the mountain: long-abandoned roads, animal trails beneath tall maples that dwarf the colonies of Scotch broom. Against a blue autumn sky, the brittle yellow leaves of the maples and the alders glitter. The air is woven with cedar-scent, and deeper in the third- or fourth-growth forest thick beds of moss are speckled with mushrooms. Sometimes the dog and I sit by the river, the rolling water murmuring like voices from the past.

..

Duran et al. delineate six phases of historical trauma specific to Indigenous communities. Under the "Boarding School Period" they say that "children were forced into a colonial lifeworld where the Native lifeworld was despised and thought of as inferior and evil." Is this the echo that passed from Great Grandmother Rosalie to my grandmother Pearl, who married three white men altogether, to my mother, who married my white father, to freckled, pale-skinned me, raised as a white woman, who also married a white man, who sees her Indigenous ancestry dissolving into an elusive past?

..

In 1958, at a British conference on tuberculosis, South Africa's top TB expert, B.A. Dormer, said, "...if any nation with limited resources at its disposal, be they financial or human, were to put its money into good food for every citizen, proper housing for every citizen, clean safe water for all, proper disposal for sewage and waste for the whole community—it could safely ignore the ever increasing demand for the provision of expensive hospitals, clinics, physicians, chemicals, antibiotics and vaccines in the campaign against tuberculosis." More than sixty years later, TB persists in the poorer communities of the world, including Indigenous communities in Canada. In 2018, Canada's chief public health officer, Theresa Tam, presented a report titled *The Time is Now*, a twenty-page appeal to finally eliminate tuberculosis in Canada, where she noted that rates of TB were forty times higher in First Nations communities and almost three hundred times higher amongst the Inuit.

..

COVID-19 enters the lungs in the same way as TB, though the former is viral, and the latter bacterial. Chronic Obstructive Pulmonary Disease, or COPD, which isn't contagious unless manifesting as certain types of pneumonia, is a group of progressive lung diseases, most commonly emphysema and bronchitis. My mother, who was a grand smoker, ultimately died of COPD. Researchers are currently investigating a genetic disposition toward this disease. A number of years ago, I was diagnosed with mild "exercise-induced" asthma. I've never been a smoker, though I lived with smokers for the better part of my life. When the dog and I go up along the old roads toward the mountain's higher peaks, sometimes a spectral hand clasps my lungs and causes me to stop to catch my breath. My limbs grow leaden, and I'm as numb as a clear-cut; I name it grief. I wish my mother were here. I think now we could talk. I'd tell her sometimes I feel as if I am the invasive species.

..

Colonialism spreads its tendrils into everything, from how we teach our children to how we care for the sick. But its tenacity is surface spread only, its substratum an illusion. There is no upending cultures whose roots have grown deep into this land for thousands of years. The Tŝilhqot'in are one of many First Nations who've taken actions to protect their communities from COVID-19. These nations have sent petitions to the government in which they've asked for jurisdiction over their own data; they've erected roadblocks to limit their communities to residents only; they've arranged vaccinations for their members and isolation for those infected with the virus. They're managing the pandemic in their territories despite barriers at the bottom of which are persistent racist attitudes. These are not the actions of victims, but the enactment of resistance, of "survivance."

..

By the afternoon the fog has lifted, and the fisherman is gone from the shore. The sun slants through the tall firs and washes the open part of the yard beyond the window. It's one of those fine fall days I love. I've been too long at my desk, and sometimes this house is a trap. I need to get outside. On my way down the stairs to the shore my eyes scan for bindweed, looking past the dune grass, the wild roses, the thimbleberry bushes and mahonia as if they're not there. Satisfied that my husband and I got most of it in August when we staged our last assault, I drop to the beach and stretch my legs out on the gravel.

That day we'd torn at the flimsy weeds through the hot morning, our arms scratched from rose thorns and our foreheads slimed with sweat. Our neighbour, with his old dog at his side, had stopped on his walk. Sinewy and tough, he was a former logger like my father.

"You'll never be rid of it," he said. He shook his head, and we agreed. He gestured toward the spade in my hand. "You don't need to dig it out. Soon as it appears above the soil, pluck the leaves. That'll weaken its roots and slow it down. Just don't give it the light."

The sea is still, a brilliant blue, and the sun warms my back. I'm wondering what it is I give the light to. We've been talking about cutting down a fir to make room for an oak that has grown from a seedling to a six-metre tree in the ten years we've lived here. This would remove the oak from the fir's shadow, allowing it more sun. The oak grows slowly, but its trunk and its limbs are muscular and gracious at the same time. Ever-lengthening branches span outwards to trace leafy patterns. It's a native tree that quietly insists on its presence, as do the histories of this land, as does the future, which we can't possibly know. We can lay in wait, steel ourselves for what may come—disease, climate disaster, deprivation—or we can grow what we have, strengthen our good roots. I close my eyes and lift my face to the sun. A breeze strokes my face, and I get to my feet.

# THE JOURNEY

# THE TEN RULES OF THE CANOE

So often we're asked to land on one side or the other: right or left, feminine or masculine, white or Indigenous. We either belong or we don't belong. Is that what this quest to reconcile the losses—my mother, an ancestral history—has been about? A desire to claim one identity or the other? I know it drove me to my participation in Tribal Canoe Journeys over three consecutive summers, from 2017 to 2019. Still, I continue to land as if on water.

..

I believe in signs. I learned this from my mother, who had dreams so vivid they were like stories, and usually stories with a message. She believed in messages, in guardian angels—mine being my long dead grandfather—and in the prophecies of teacup readers. Sometimes she would phone and ask me if there'd been an accident, some marital trouble or an unexpected visitor. It was alarming how often her hunches were bang on. "A feeling," she'd say, "I just had a feeling." My mother's deep intuitive nature and her belief in the ineffable were dismissed as superstition, scoffed at by my father and the world. Yet, in some ways, my trust in the so-called universe has always been the secret well from which I've drawn. I've come to believe the universe, whoever, whatever that might be—*cosmic energy, Buddha, my creator or my long dead grandfather, God*—circles back with that which it wants us to heed. I received three such messages regarding Tribal Journeys before I was able to welcome them for the invitation they were.

The first came from a young W̱SÁNEĆ woman I'd met in my role as an outreach worker sometime in the mid-nineties. She was excited to be going on a canoe journey with members of her community, and she invited me to come along. Though I can't recall exactly where they were headed, I learned from her that they would join other Indigenous communities from all over the Pacific Northwest to eventually gather in a "host community." There, for several days, they would share traditional songs and dances. Despite my intrigue and faint hope that the trip would connect me to my lost Coast Salish heritage, an old ambivalence reared in me, a pull to claim and at the same time to deny the Indigenous ancestry that I feared wasn't rightfully mine. With my freckled skin I would have only been exposed as the imposter I surely was. Regardless, I'll never forget this young woman and her passion, not only for her child, who she fought to keep from the clutches of child welfare, but also for her culture, and because she's the first who made me aware of Tribal Journeys.

..

The canoe journeys were initiated by Elder Emmet Oliver with the Paddle to Seattle in 1989 for the Washington State centenary. Forty canoes from several Washington tribes and Canadian First Nations took to the water, some in traditional cedar canoes built for the occasion. Though canoe travel had once been at the heart of Northwest Coast Indigenous culture, the colonialist assault on cultural practices brought it largely to an end. In 1989, some communities paddled for the first time in one hundred years.

..

Several years after the young woman from Saanich made me aware of Tribal Canoe Journeys, a second sign came to me from the universe. By that time, I was living in a house on Baynes Sound in the Comox Valley where the ocean trained my eye toward itself. The first summer after the move, I caught sight of a half-dozen canoes travelling north along Denman Island. The rhythm of the pullers' voices singing the old songs travelled on the wind and the waves across the sound. Stumbling over the rocks to the low-tide line with binoculars in hand, I felt a yearning to be in the canoe.

..

In 1989 Frank Brown from the Heiltsuk Nation issued a challenge to those canoe families gathered in Seattle to paddle to Bella Bella in 1993. From there the Tribal Canoe Journeys eventually became an annual event that has attracted thousands of people, with Indigenous representation from as far away as New Zealand. In recent years it's been common for over one hundred canoes to assemble at the host community where the final protocol is held. They are accompanied by up to 12,000 participants who come as ground crew, support boat crew, dancers, singers, family and friends. The community is engaged in a myriad of hosting activities from traffic control to cooking for thousands of people. Paddlers travel for days stopping as guests of various nations/tribes along the way for food and rest until they arrive at their destination, where they partake in several days of cultural sharing.

..

My third invitation came in 2014 after a neighbourhood friend, who had affiliations with the local First Nation, brought me along to a practice paddle at Qualicum First Nation in the canoe called *The Singing Coho*. I'd told my friend about my Indigenous ancestry, and how years earlier I'd visited a W̱SÁNEĆ cousin who sketched a family tree for me. I still recall the speed of her pencil despite going back two or three generations, all that history in her head. Soon after that visit, I dropped my research for several years—though to this day I cherish that creased and faded piece of paper, a root to all I've discovered since.

Immediately after the practice, while sitting with the group of a dozen or so participants laughing, snacking and talking, the skipper invited me to return. At the time my mother was dying, and I'd recently started a demanding job. I wasn't yet ready to make room for the journey in my life.

Two years later my friend explained that the host community for 2017 Tribal Journey would be in Campbell River, territory of the Ligwiłda'xw people, a southern tribe of the Kwakwaka'wakw people, only an hour's drive from where we lived, and because it was close to where we lived, she thought it might make the trip more possible for me. *The Singing Coho* canoe, a many-nations, all-ages canoe, would be paddling from Qualicum to Campbell River with a crew of ideally twenty-four paddlers from their community. Others would go along, not to paddle but to offer support and to participate in the cultural sharing, and some would volunteer to help with the road crew. Me, I would maybe paddle, help where I could. I just wanted to be there, finally. Invisible, perhaps, in the way my mother's ancestry had been invisible, in the way I preferred to be in crowds, as if I were not really there. Did I think that I might slide into this unacknowledged history unnoticed?

..

The Ten Rules of the Canoe, which lay out the guiding principles for expected behaviour on a canoe journey, were developed by Tom Heidlebaugh and David Forlines during a 1990 educational conference in Washington State. On the journey in 2017, I received a small card listing the rules with a brief commentary on each. Some days, I remove it from where it's tacked above my desk, and read it again, as if to understand it in a new way.

## 1. EVERY STROKE WE TAKE IS ONE LESS WE HAVE TO MAKE
*Each pull forward is real movement and not delusion.*

This journey begins with sound, one blade stroke on a skinless sea. Swish. The evening sun pauses on the horizon, as if listening. Voices in an ancient tongue rise in song from the mouths of the paddlers and skip across the ocean's surface. It might be the canoe itself that sings. My mother is dying. A kingfisher's rattle and whirr of wing-flap as it spins toward the water. These images are what I remember most about that first practice. It will be two years before I circle back. In so many ways, we live always with the desire for return.

## 2. THERE IS TO BE NO ABUSE OF SELF OR OTHERS
*Respect and trust cannot exist in anger. It has to be thrown overboard, so the sea can cleanse it.*

One winter, I taught English as a second language to a group of landed immigrants three nights a week in a small north island community, and because of a computer glitch my attendance records were erased. I felt an unreasonable amount of despair over this. I think it was because I knew my students had been there night after night, breathing, talking, laughing, succeeding, failing. I knew it in the way you know in your body that their bodies in flesh and blood were present, struggling nightly toward articulation. Isn't all of life, its inadequate articulations, its record keeping, gestures toward affirming our presence?

During that particularly cold winter, the locals told me to be aware of the black ice on the highway home. "It's invisible," they said, "sneaks up on you." It was late by the time I left one night, and since the road was deserted, and I was anxious for a cup of tea and bed, I allowed my speed to ramp upward. I was lucky. Though aware that the ice could grab the tires of a car and spin it off course, I put it out of my mind. Such is the danger of erasure.

..

My mother put her Coast Salish ancestry out of her mind, and in those white suburbs in which I grew up there seemed no need to mention it.

..

In the Qualicum canoe, I'm surrounded by younger pullers, more at ease with their sense of belonging than I, with their cousins on board and their strong limbs.

I paddle only on easy days, but one such day the sea goes restless and we land hard on the sand beach. The canoe is too heavy to lift, so we drag it above the tide line. That night the skipper says, "You all have your reasons for coming on the journey. Don't make the canoe heavy with the weight in your heart. Give it up to the water."

## 3. BE FLEXIBLE
*When the wind confronts you, sometimes you're supposed to go the other way.*

What I want on this first journey is to paddle in tandem with the pullers, straight to Ligwiłda'xw territory, which by car is a straight and brief trip on Highway 19—one hour. I know nothing of the distance by water. I want to take my place on the canoe like the newcomers to this land, those also in my ancestry, wanted what they assumed was theirs. Though I'm not accomplished, I've learned to immerse the paddle straight into the water and pull, to ply and to draw, to meet the water without touching the blade in front of me, to follow its return, to find that rhythm. I've learned technique, though I'm not strong, and I don't paddle as if I'm an arm of one being. I'm me, with aching shoulders and a regret I haven't trained with push-ups. I'm driven by a fear of failure.

..

How the sea carries the canoe is dependent on the swirl of ocean around the curve and jut of land, on its deep currents, on tides and on the weather above its surface. The sea that thrashes and deceives also mobilizes and soothes, behaves like a two-headed serpent. It brings death while also teeming with life. Sisiutl, as the serpent is named, might transform into a fish or a canoe. And it stands for duality, the one half in conflict with the other.

My mother had an unremitting fear of snakes her entire life, was known, out of some unarticulated imagined terror, to cleave them in half with a garden shovel.

In her book *Celia's Song*, novelist Lee Maracle describes the battle between the double-headed sea serpent in which one head bites off the other. This severance unleashes a violence in the community, specifically toward a woman and her child. It underlines the division that has existed for two hundred years between the white and Indigenous communities. My grandmother was split off from her Coast Salish roots, and therefore, so was my mother. This unseen violence wrote both their life stories and lingers in mine.

..

The first time I dance to drums I wear a borrowed cape from the K'ómoks people, on whose territory we are guests. I try to think of the drumbeat as a knock on the door, an invitation, but the cape only goes to my bare knees just above my MEC nylon shorts and I feel like the one who wasn't invited. No door opens. It's a summer of wildfires, and the moon is blood red in a smoke-smudged sky.

Despite what I want, that night I'm told that I will not be paddling the next day. I've learned from my mother to say nothing and hold my head high. In the morning before daybreak, I crowd into a car with several others and am driven to the harbour. Though I've been there many times, in the dark and the mist with the flurry of activity it's not a harbour I know. Another woman and I, along with five youth ranging in age from about ten to seventeen years old, board a boat that will spend the day supporting a few of the canoes paddling north, including *The Singing Coho*. Dampness from the air and the sea enter my bones. Somewhere, far beneath the cloud cover, the scorched red sun rises over a strange land.

On the support boat the woman, who is named Candice, and I laugh and talk with the children. We ensure that they eat and that they're safe. This I can do; I have children of my own, grown now. We welcome the pullers from the other canoes who come aboard for rest. They share their food with us as we've somehow left our cooler on the dock at the harbour. We laugh at our forgetfulness and scan the sea for *The Singing Coho*. Into the afternoon, we settle on the upper deck of the boat. The sea is calm, and the sky thinly overcast. My new friend is a lavish woman with silver whales dangling from her ears, a cedar hat on her head and multicolour beads hanging around her neck. She speaks with gusto and good humour. Beside her, in my practical MEC zip-up jacket and hiking pants, and with my reticence and cut-up carrots, I'm aware of my own meagreness. But as the afternoon wears on we laugh again and tell stories of our mothers, our ex-husbands and lovers, our children. As for our troubles, though she's had to be stronger than me, in the end they aren't so different.

Closer to Campbell River, whirlpools swirl around the boat. More and more canoes appear, the pullers paddling hard to negotiate currents and rising wind, voices rising in song over the water. Still, there's been no word of our canoe. We fear an accident, someone hurt, and as illogical and impossible as it is, we also fear that we've been cast out from our canoe family. We've both lived long enough to know well this admixture of fears. We're weary with it by the end of the day when the captain steers the boat into the passage where the tide running north off Vancouver Island clashes with that running south. We bounce across the turbulent currents to the dock where *The Singing Coho* arrived hours before. We know not to ask questions, to only listen as the day's events are revealed over time. We disembark, and Candice, now a friend, shrugs and says, "This is the journey."

## 4. THE GIFT OF EACH ENRICHES ALL
*Everyone is part of the movement.*

Candice brings herself as the gift. If she knew the cancer cells were dividing in her at the time, she said nothing to me. I didn't know what my gift to her or to the journey was. I suspect I was a taker, a woman raised white.

During the week of protocol, between the sharing of story, dance and song in the big house, she leads me to the place where there is to be a copper ring ceremony. The man who makes the rings introduces himself as Philip Red Eagle. He says, "I want to make enough for everyone, but today I only have so many rings. Some of you were not invited." He's a big man with a warm voice, and he appears more concerned than annoyed.

"I'm one who wasn't invited," I volunteer.

"I thought you looked strange," he says, and I nod, knowing this to be the truth of my presence here—though I want to reply, *You mean estranged*. I don't. He invites me to stay.

Candice and I, older by several years than the many young people present, sit in chairs. They gather on the ground beneath the small canopy, grow silent. The man begins by passing on the history of Tribal Journeys. An older man seated next to him nods through the telling, clarifies a few details, and shares a joke or two. The rest of us are rapt as if gathered around a kitchen table where we are meant to hear something both personal and vital.

After he teaches this history, he hands each of us the Ten Rules of the Canoe transcribed onto a small card and selects some of us to read out loud. It's my turn to read when we get to number three: *Be flexible*. What had I expected to find on the journey: my mother, my grandmother, a missing part of myself, to know finally the place from which we'd been banished, or banished ourselves, or internalized our banishment, through the mechanisms of assimilationist policies and attitudes, and to be welcomed in a warm embrace as if we were not strangers. *The adaptable animal survives. If you get tired, ship your paddle and rest*, I read.

..

On that first journey, I sleep in a large tent with three adolescent youth. We choose to leave the tent fly off so we can stare up through the mesh ceiling and look for the stars deep within the smoky sky. Each evening, I return from the big house after the last canoe family has shared for the day, but I don't sleep until I know all three have crawled into their beds, until I've said *good night*. I begin to think this, at least, I can give.

..

I no longer look from the ocean below my home without imagining the ghosts of canoes from another time retracing their ancestral paths. The vision of Coast Salish ancestors on their summer journeys arises as if it were a long-forgotten memory. History turned memory may be the best gift I can give that first journey, while also being the best I can receive.

## 5. WE ALL PULL AND SUPPORT EACH OTHER
*When we know that we are not alone in our actions, we also know we are lifted up by everyone else.*

Two pullers told me that once on a journey they paddled with a strong crew, but the day had been long and hard. All they could think of was one thrust of the blade after the other. They didn't say who was there or the time of day, nor did they mention the weather conditions. Only that the canoe rose above the water. It seemed natural at the time, the sea and the forward momentum, the wind, the arms of all the pullers pulling in unison, their mind, one mind. Their combined effort lifted the canoe and for a moment they flew above the water.

Tom Heidlebaugh says in the afterword for David Neel's book *The Great Canoes*: "...the canoe participates in the sea, riding the waves and carving through the roll like a pilot whale. It's sometimes airborne, sometimes as stable as its aboriginal tree."

## 6. A HUNGRY PERSON HAS NO CHARITY
*The gift of who you are only enters the world when you are strong enough to own it.*

At times it's a challenge to stay nourished on the journey. I devour food as if I've been famished for a long time. I gobble cold thin burgers (though I eat no red meat as a rule), soggy salmon sandwiches on white bread that dissolve on the tongue, salty oolichan, fistfuls of clams off the mound above the firepit and sweet, doughy bannock. I'm greedy for satiation, not only from food but from the pulse and colour of dance and drumbeat. N. Scott Momaday, the Kiowa writer, says in *House Made of Dawn* that the drum is "...like the breaking of thunder far away, echoing on and on in a region out of time." Throughout the days of the journey, the drum is constant: the beat participates in my dreams.

## 7. EXPERIENCES ARE NOT ENHANCED THROUGH CRITICISM
*Withdrawing the blame acknowledges how wonderful a part of it all every one of us really is.*

On the second journey, the following year, my husband and I volunteer for road crew. Though we're responsible for welcoming *The Singing Coho* at the final landing place and transporting our paddlers to the campsite, we're late, and it turns out we've picked the wrong campsite. We purchase cheap white bread on which I make soggy sandwiches at midnight in the pouring rain. When we're given the responsibility of leading an elder, who follows us in her car along the Washington highways, to the host community, we lose her somewhere on the I-5 then drive in circles on back roads before we get to our destination. The elder hasn't yet arrived.

..

Though small in stature, my mother was a strong woman who could have carried a deer carcass on her back, or blankets, pots and pans. At work, she lifted trays weighted with meat for the butchers, and at home she heaved a vacuum cleaner, dragged an ironing board and once, in a rage, flung a full bag of garbage across the kitchen. She was known to do the same to an untidy pile of shoes by the door, so that sometimes our front lawn sprouted a crop of random footwear. Anger surged in her, generated the energy she needed to keep going—or was it love all along? She could have lifted a car off a child, and she would have for her children.

..

On that second journey the elder, sensing discord amongst our canoe family, asks for a circle, and it helps to quell the complaints, the surge of anger. I miss my friend from the first canoe trip who would have said, "It's the journey."

On my way home to my house by the sea I tell myself I will not go back, but the heart wants a return.

## 8. THE JOURNEY IS WHAT WE ENJOY
*Being on the journey, we are much more than ourselves.*

A journey can't happen without baggage, however big or small. We cart memory around as if it were a rollie suitcase. One night my brother who died too young appears in my dream.

"What's all the excitement?" he asks.

Seeing him, I'm as full of happiness as a balloon is full of air. "I didn't know you wanted to go on the journey with me," I say. Sometimes, we bring the dead along with us. In the big house, I spot the back of my long-deceased grandmother's head, cropped hair, dyed black with grey roots, on a squat yet muscular body, disappearing through the crowd.

I have conversations with my deceased mother, explain to her why I'm here, because she acts as if I've betrayed her, as if I've exposed a deeply buried part of herself. I say, *The richness of this culture is your birthright.*

*Not mine*, she says and covers her eyes as she was accustomed to doing her whole life. I doubt myself, ask why I'm here, as if my mother and me are one and the same. Then I catch a glimpse of a woman with my mother's slight build, her eyes warm with joy, dancing with the women to the drums, and her voice lifts above the others in song.

..

Much to my relief a few hours after we've lost her the elder shows up. I apologize and buy her and her granddaughter lemonade. She's mostly silent and doesn't say it's okay because it's not, exactly. She does allow us to help put up her tent. I feel clumsy around her. After dinner I watch a younger woman slide a brush through the elder's waist-length hair. The women talk softly as the younger one gathers the elder's hair in her hand, divides it into three strands and weaves one over the other. She does this with such love and attention, I want someone, someday, to braid my hair in that way.

"I can't grow mine long," I blurt, and they look up, startled at my voice as if they've forgotten I'm there. I'm fighting back tears. It's been such a difficult day.

"You have to let it get past the difficult stage," says the elder. Her eyes are soft in the evening light.

On the day we lost the elder, we camp in a community next to a large outdoor sports stadium. In the early evening, guttural shouts and screams erupt from that direction below where we camp. Some of us rush toward the noise expecting to witness a violent confrontation. Out on the field under the bright stadium lights, a line of men, half naked with painted faces, crouch on their haunches with their tongues hanging out. They abruptly turn and jump; each sound from their mouths is a detonation.

"It's the Maoris," someone shouts, and laughter ripples through the crowd. We press against the chain-link fence that borders the field, fixated on the threat we hear in the *haka*.

Throughout the night the stadium lights wash over our encampment while my husband and I try to sleep in our tiny pup tent. Outside its nylon walls hundreds of people mill about, laughing, talking and singing in tongues unknown to us, and the drum beats like hammer and nail throughout the night. Inside our tent, we bicker in whispers. It's not that we're frightened. It's that we're amidst an electrical impulse that can't be explained by youthfulness or resistance, though it's both. We're in the middle of something so big we come face to face with our smallness.

## 9. A GOOD TEACHER ALLOWS THE STUDENT TO LEARN
*Each paddler learns to deal with the person in front, the person behind, the water, the air, the energy, the blessing of the eagle.*

On the third journey, in the third year, we get it right—though not without the presence of and much assistance from Auntie Carrie. We erect the tents before the pullers get in, and we are there on the shore to greet them. The sandwiches are not soggy. I'm invited to paddle with them on the day we land at W̱SÁNEĆ, the home of my grandmothers. No one from my lineage or who otherwise knows me waits on the shore. Their absence, I begin to realize, is something I can live with.

## 10. WHEN GIVEN ANY CHOICE AT ALL, BE A WORKER BEE— MAKE HONEY!

On that first journey when we go north to Campbell River we sit beneath the canopy where Philip Red Eagle makes the rings and gives a teaching. Afterwards he stands, drapes the necklaces he's made hours before over his hand and steps around the circle, stopping to give one to each person present. When he gets to me, I remind him I wasn't invited, therefore, I won't take one. He shakes his head and says, "You came, and you stayed." He places the necklace around my neck. I roll its single bead between my fingers.

After the second journey and before the third my friend Candice from the support boat dies from cancer. Despite saying I would, I hadn't kept in touch, though I sent her a brief message when I heard she was ill. She responded with a thank-you and a promise that we'd *make memories together again in the future*. It turns out that we won't in this life, but on that third journey, with the necklace tucked under my shirt against my flesh, on our pull into W̱SÁNEĆ, I imagine her there on the beach standing next to the ghosts of my grandmothers and my mother, all of them barefoot on the sand, arms outspread as if to welcome me, not home, but to this place where I've landed.

Jordan Abel in *NISHGA* says, "I also wrote this book because I thought I could write my way home... It turns out that wasn't the case... I didn't find my way anywhere but deeper."

I have work to do, to understand what it means to grieve, to claim a place or to live without a claim to a place no longer mine. The journey is not over after three trips in the canoe. Maybe it's never over.

# Permission to Land

The heat from the noonday sun permeates to the bone, and the ocean shifts beneath me. My heart beats with the drums on the shore. I'm at the back of the canoe two seats up from the skipper. "Now?" I ask him. He nods and looks toward the beach. Like déjà vu I have a feeling I've been here before, and yet I know much has changed in my absence.

..

It's difficult to pinpoint when a journey begins. Is it when the canoe first touches the water, the paddle penetrates the sea, months before at the fundraiser when the profits are counted and the expenses calculated—or is it years before, when the ancestors of your black-haired, dark-eyed mother indwell the edges of your childhood? Is it later when you discover that there are First Nations cultures going on without you, despite your ancestors belonging to those cultures? You feel excluded, yet you need only look at your freckled skin to know that you have no rightful claim to it after two generations' absence?

Maybe the journey's commencement clarion was sounded the moment your great-great-grandmothers became wives to Scottish blacksmiths, then went on to live with a crippling shame for not being good enough white women, which they passed on to the women in your line? You discover all this early enough in your life, but you do nothing until your mother dies and you feel like you've always felt, that there's something you need to do for her that you're not doing.

..

One week to the day before my mother died, a raven flew through the open patio doors into my house. I hid in the hallway until moments later when it flew back out the same doors. As my mother and my auntie would have done, I chose to take it as a sign.

..

When things go wrong—such as crossed communication, milk soured in the cooler, something left behind, an overpowering sense of guilt or grief, elation, sore muscles—and dreams punctuated with drumbeat and story reverberate in the mind for days after the return home, the pullers, the organizers, and the road crew call it "the journey."

..

I've discovered that there is no beginning, middle and end to this journey. I've learned something about First Nations culture but, more importantly, about myself and who I am within my ancestral history, so I've begun to think of my return to the annual cultural event as a circling into my personal reconciliation with a past that coalesces with the present. Grief, too, necessitates a return, and with each orbit our relationship with the deceased is made anew. Absence has taught me a new way of knowing my mother and my grandmothers.

..

In the canoe with the sun beating on me, I'm telling my mother about the journey. "This is it," I say to her. This is the moment when I ask to open a door, a door that has long been closed to my mother and my grandmothers. All day between the paddle strokes, behind the voices singing across the water and in the music of the waves, they are here, but as incorporeal as humming. They have been this way for a long time, though they've never been so loud. I hear them over the roar of motorboats.

..

My mother once told me the sea has a heartbeat. Like the raven, I took it as a sign that I should pay attention to the sea. I wrote it down so I wouldn't forget. I've forgotten so much.

..

Moments before this moment, we were lagging after several hours of paddling, and as we angled toward the beach, we came alongside another canoe full of pullers from the north who challenged us to a race. Competition—though that's not what the journey is about—woke us up and we did twenty hard pulls then thirty hard pulls until we overcame the other canoe. We were laughing when we approached Tsawout, one of the five Saanich First Nations.

..

North of Tsawout two nights before, we were hosted by the Snuneymuxw First Nation, well fed, and invited out of the rain to sleep in the home of one of their members. Their reserve sits on a long sandy beach that faces Harmac, a pulp mill that has a production capacity of 365,000 tonnes of pulp per year. This makes the clams unsafe to eat. Snuneymuxw First Nation has a pre-Confederation treaty and is one of the largest First Nations in British Columbia, but its treaty rights have been so consistently violated by the Crown that 1,700 people live on the smallest reserve land base per capita of any nation in BC.

My DNA is as much in the filth that drains from Harmac into the Salish Sea as it is in the Saanich Inlet where my grandmothers once paddled. I don't have this feeling of grief and connection for my European ancestors, though, because I can't find their ancient histories and songs in this land where I've lived all my life, the traditional territory of the Coast Salish.

..

I'd hoped the canoes would be lined up along the shore, and one by one they would ask for permission to land so that I'd know what to say when it was my turn, but there's only one canoe who arrived moments before us, and I can't hear what is said. The one we raced with slides in to shore on our other side just as I struggle to my feet. My fellow paddlers hold the canoe steady for me.

..

At lunchtime, we'd tied our canoe to the support boat, and the crew had leaned over the side and handed us sandwiches, cookies and fruit. Sitting in the canoe, we chattered about the morning's paddle and ate while it rocked gently, and the sea sparkled around us.

Before we set out again, our skipper said, "Judy will ask for permission to land."

A couple of the younger women who knew Saanich was home to my ancestors smiled at me, and I smiled back, flooded with gratitude—then trepidation. "What should I say?"

"Speak from your heart," the skipper said. Though he's younger than my son, in that moment I have this feeling about the skipper I sometimes do with the elders, that he knows something about me that I don't yet know.

All day I imagined the past. That's all you can do with the past, isn't it? I mean the past before you were born. Then there's that other past, all the things that happened since you were born, things you've either forgotten or for which you had no understanding at the time, as when you were a child, and you woke to the sounds of your parents' voices. It wasn't the words you heard, only the knife edge of your father's intonation, the sound of your mother crying. As if there'd been no passage of time, something coils in your belly even now. In this way, the past isn't a fixed bygone phenomenon, but as artist, writer and scholar Leanne Betasamosake Simpson says, "the present... is a colliding of the past and the future."

Earlier in the morning we'd had to rest our paddles and wait for the ferry to depart at Swartz Bay, where it would cross our path. Ours and two other canoes were dwarfed by the vessel, the queen of something because they're all called queens, a behemoth, white and sparkly against the blue water. I imagined people behind the massive windows staring at us from the vessel's insect eyes. We were quiet, rocking in a gentle roller. "Look stoic," said the young woman who sat nearer the bow and who'd dropped over the side earlier to cool off. We all laughed.

..

There are two men on the shore from the Tsawout First Nation who are greeting the canoes. They've just invited the canoe that landed seconds before us, and their pullers are climbing out and preparing to carry the canoe out of the water. There is little fanfare, and the greeters aren't wearing regalia as they sometimes are at landings. They have a job to do; people are landing and they're going to be looking for places to camp and eat. There could be hundreds of people by now. At every stop more canoes join those paddling farther south to Lummi Island in Washington State.

I've hesitated too long. The men on the shore look at me then at one another. They talk quietly. I'm a teacher. I know how to do this though I usually plan carefully. I'm surrounded on the canoe by people who have my back. And I'm trying to find my heart, from which I've been told to speak.

..

Beyond the ferry we passed several marinas lined with yachts and large powerboats. Where there aren't marinas, enormous houses clutch the shoreline. In front of them slope green lawns, sometimes bordered by stat-ues and exotic plants. Apartment complexes with little balconies protrude over the water. James Island, once Tsawout land, now owned by a Seattle billionaire, comes into view.

I try to envision this waterway in a time before the giant houses and the private land, the roar of engine and industry, in a past when elegant arbutus leaned from the rocky banks along the shore while the dense forest behind teemed with life, and the waters were abundant with fish, and there was silence except for the cry of a raven above and the stirring of the ocean beneath the canoe. In that moment the skipper breaks into a song in the Hul'q'umi'num' tongue and the sound of drumbeat rolls across the water. I'm overcome with grief for the loss of memory, and for the stories I never knew, for my mother, and for the theft that occurred in this place.

..

The men are looking in my direction. They wait. My canoe family sits with the blade of their paddles pointing up, also waiting. I usually speak too quietly for people and my words disappear, but I've learned to project my voice over a classroom. I tell the men my first name and I say who I'm paddling with. "We've had a wonderful morning paddling through your waters. My great-grandmother came from Saanich, and I'm happy to be here. We are tired and hungry and ask to come ashore and share food and song with you."

..

Until a few moments before, I'd never seen Mt. Newton from the water, and as we passed, I recalled a story told to me by a W̱SÁNEĆ cousin, which I've also seen in other sources. When all the land now called Saanich was covered with flood waters the people climbed into their canoes and tied them to an arbutus tree whose top branches were exposed above the water. This was the sacred mountain, ȽÁU, WELṈEW—meaning *place of refuge*—what is now known as Mt. Newton. When the water finally began to recede, Raven circled around an emerging piece of land and a young child called to her people. An elder pointed to the land and repeated what the child said, "W̱SÁNEĆ," and added "our new home."

..

When I finish with my request, the men fall into discussion with one another. Water laps against the canoe, and the other pullers shift in their seats. I want to flee, to go back again. Surely, they will turn me down and I'll humiliate my canoe family members.

"Welcome to our shore," says one of the men.

For a second, I hesitate, fearful I will prove an imposter, my grandmother and mother's long denial now so much a part of me. But there's no going back. My canoe family pounds the grips of their upturned paddles on the canoe's belly beneath their feet. I step over the gunwale and wade in the shallow water toward a beach where my grandmothers once walked. I mouth the SENĆOŦEN word for the Saanich people, W̱SÁNEĆ, which in English means *emerging*.

# Sacred Process

This hat has known another life: first as a seedling then as the bark of a tree, from which it was separated by the sharp blade and the loving hands of its maker, an elder weaver. Woven of cedar strips that trace a flat crown and a wide brim, it's drawn together by a band with a diagonal that holds three crow's feathers. The colour varies across the weave between red, yellow and brown, shifting according to the light. Auntie Carrie, who once wore it on her head, has given it to me. It's mine, for now—this gift of the forest.

..

The business of giving was complicated for my family; perhaps this is so for all families. Photographs of Christmas in the sixties when my brothers, sister and I were kids depict piles of gifts under the tree, bulging, spilling onto the carpet, my mother in a flowery housecoat curled into a corner of the couch, coffee in hand, exhaustion straining her smile. Our gifts weren't expensive but they were plentiful and sumptuously wrapped in shiny paper. Our living room was a diorama of Christmas in the 1960s, the tree glittering with tinsel. My sister and I received dolls and pretty dresses, my brothers trucks and toy guns. At Sunday school we were told the story of the birth of Jesus, and at home the one about Santa Claus sliding down the chimney. Acquisition and its accumulation made it a nerve-tingling time of excitement, always hovering at a tipping point where joy risked catapulting into disappointment, something manic and unlevel about the mood in the house.

..

Before I was given the cedar hat, I bought a hat from Cabela's, that box chain store that sells guns, fishing rods and all manner of outdoor gear, with a plan to wear it on the Tribal Canoe Journey in July 2019. It was lightweight, and I thought it would be good protection from the sun. The hat is made of polyester, a synthetic petroleum product.

..

For my birthday my daughter gave me a piece of cedar wood that had been carved into a spiral shape. She'd bought it from an artisan on one of the islands. We hung it on the front porch. Long before this land was my yard, the Pentlatch people—who were nearly wiped out by smallpox and war, but only nearly—walked here beneath cedars at a time when cedars grew to be hundreds and hundreds of years old. Sometimes I stand beneath my daughter's gift and with my eyes follow the interchange of breeze and light as the carving spirals into the deep, silent history of its wood.

..

Cedar bark protects and nurtures the tree by dividing its cells and sending a nutriment tissue called phloem to the outside of the tree, and xylem, a wood tissue, to the inside. In this way the bark is a borderland in which nourishment is exchanged. This is what it means to be a grandmother. My twin grandsons are a gift.

..

One time, when I came into some money, I bought my mother a computer for her small home-based garden shop. When I unpacked the box on my parents' dining room table Mom cried, "Oh no," and sprinted through the kitchen and laundry room out the door and into the yard. "Take it back, take it back," she shouted as she ran along the garden path toward the forest in the back of their place. A few minutes later she returned to the house, where I sat collapsed at the kitchen table. She touched my shoulder and said "It's too much money, Hon."

At Dad's urging, I left the computer with them anyway, and it was he who learned to use it, and with his help, sometimes Mom would email us, but other than that she would have nothing to do with my gift. It might have been the technology that frightened her because it's not that she didn't believe in gift giving. She taught me that it was bad luck to go to someone's house without something to give. For her grandchildren she often brought chocolate chip cookies, and for me a plant dug from her garden and flowers. Somehow for my mother the receiving end of the transaction was severed.

..

The inner layer of bark, which is used for weaving, is called the vascular cambium. It's the part that forms the rings we count on a cut tree to determine its age. Pliable and smooth, after cutting it into strips then soaking it in water, it's the perfect malleability to manoeuvre into woven fabric.

In the documentary *Story of Cedar, Cedar Hat Weaving and Bark Pulling*, Maria Sampson, a cedar weaver, says there is "a sacred process when the land offers a part of itself to help you with your life and those are the kinds of things I'm thinking about when I'm asking that tree to give some of its skin."

..

*Extractivism* is a word Leanne Betasamosake Simpson says means the opposite of giving, and the basis of the colonial mentality: "It's stealing. It's taking something... out of the relationships that give it meaning." Simpson captures the alternative to extractivism in the phrase "deep reciprocity," which consists of "respect... relationship... responsibility." This is the spirit in which the cedar hat was given to me, one in which the gift was not freighted with an expectation of a thank-you so much as an invitation to commit to relationship.

..

Generosity is the first perfection according to Mahayana Buddhism. Giving freely without expectation is a way to practise compassion and non-attachment. I have a friend who walks past the unhoused in our country emptying a pocketful of change into their hands. She never speculates on how the money will be spent. For her, the act of giving is unconditional.

On a trip through Tibet, our guide requested that we not make beggars of his people. We were in the famous Barkhor Square where shoppers swarmed amongst devotees who wore kneepads and prostrated toward the Jokhang Temple under the hot August sun. When two young boys asked me for money, I recalled the guide's request and diverted their attention by complimenting their English and asking them questions about school. They showed me their schoolbooks. The Chinese want everyone to learn English, even the Tibetans. The English language is spread around Tibet like a commodity. It's said to be the language of commerce and infects like a virus.

When the boys left, I noticed an old woman nearby who sat on a stone bench outside the temple. Her hair, pulled into a ponytail, was traced with grey. She wore a blouse stained at the collar and a threadbare skirt. She must have heard me talking to the children. Rather than looking into my face, she turned her ear toward my voice, a gesture of someone who is blind or near blind. She held both palms out. "Please," she said. A small empty bowl rested on her lap. She removed her sunglasses and pointed to her eyes, both clouded with a milky puddle. The sun was fierce over the Tibetan Plateau and above the city. "Please," she said again. I clutched a few yuan notes in the pocket of my shorts, running through my mind our guide's request not to *make beggars*... My group had amassed a short distance away. "Lunch," my husband mouthed, and beckoned. I shook my head at the woman with the cataracted eyes, walked away clutching the money in my pocket. I think of her from time to time, and I'm consumed with shame.

..

The story of the man who at his death was transformed into the first red cedar is told by some Coast Salish people. This man was resourceful and cared for his people by always providing them with what they needed. Frances Nahanni from the Squamish Nation says in the video *Story of Cedar* that the creator saw that this man was "good, caring, sharing and loving" and that these are the ways we all should be. So, the cedar is called the Tree of Life because it gave and continues to give so much to Coastal First Nations.

It was used for medicine and healing and it was said that if a person stood with his or her back to the tree, they could gain its strength. Sometimes, I touch the trunks of cedars. I spread the palm of my hand across the thick bark. I close my eyes and feel a blast of energy running from the trunk into my body. It's the same on a full moon night when I stand on the shore and with my eyes follow the path of the moon along the water and up to the bright orb in the sky. There is energy, if only you turn in to it. Tune in to it.

..

On the journey one sweltering July day, Auntie Carrie loaned me her hat. "Suits you," she said. I wore the hat until the sun went down.

..

The nature of the potlatch is that of giving back and forth. It is a complex economic system steeped in cultural practice and has been integral to coastal First Nations for thousands of years. It was banned between 1884 and 1951. Sixty-seven years. The only way colonialism can conceive of the practice of potlatch is through language like *squander* and *waste*, and *irresponsibility*. The early colonialists believed First Nations people needed protection from themselves. In this way they justified the potlatch ban, though really the ban was one of several strategies aimed at eliminating Indigenous people and culture.

The piece I remember most from *Potlatch 67-67: The Potlatch Ban— Then and Now*, a show at the Comox Valley Art Gallery, is an installation by Liz Carter, an artist of Kwakwaka'wakw ancestry, entitled *Renunciation #4*. A small school desk made of broken copper sits in a dimly lit room. Attached to it is an intravenous bag and pole. Lines in white chalk in neat, even cursive are written on a chalkboard. They are like those lines misbehaving children were given in public schools at one time, only here one cannot help thinking of residential schools. The surprise, however, is the words that make up these lines: *I will not feel shame. I will sing. I will dance...*

..

When I moved out at age seventeen my mother gave me a framed landscape she'd painted in a beginner's art class: a beach scene with a few driftwood logs strewn on the shore, some trees lining the bank. Benign and soothing on the wall of my first apartment, a ground level suite, knowing my mother's hand was in it, the painting offered reassurance that first year away from home. This I remember. As for what happened to the painting, it may have been stolen when my apartment was broken into, or I may have given it away, as I did the guitar my parents bought for me when I was a teenager. In those days I wanted to be a folk singer. Somewhere along the way after moving out, then dropping guitar lessons and the two college courses I was taking, I didn't anticipate "doing" anything except occasionally making it to work. It's during that bad period I gave the guitar to someone, and my mother's painting went missing. My mother knew I liked the painting and that it made me proud of her, and that's why she gave it to me. I wish I had it now. I wish I hadn't hurt her by losing it.

The gift I remember most from my mother is the one she gave me on Mother's Day shortly after my marriage split and I was an exhausted, self-punishing single mom. It was a bouquet of flowers. I don't remember what species or colour or arrangement, but I remember the attached note: *Thank-you for being such a good mother to my grandchildren.*

..

In her artist's statement Liz Carter quotes Gerald Vizenor's term "survivance" to speak not of resilience, which comes from steeling oneself against something to survive, but of a forward thrust, a thriving. She says, "The Native Warrior of Survivance is the continuance or stories in the present." You could say that the practice of giving and receiving in the potlatch creates a momentum, a rhythm, a sense of continuance. And you could say such is the nature of the act of giving, which involves receiving.

..

The roots of the cedar trees that grow in our yard have cracked and pushed the pavement in the driveway upward. You can kill a cedar, but you can never own a cedar. You can't even fence a cedar in.

..

A hat is a crowning achievement. A hat completes a face. It protects from the elements. It binds you to the elements, especially a cedar hat. A hat can be part of a uniform. It represents officialdom, authority. Hats, like words, are signifiers. A cap worn backward is a young man, handsome, physically strong, who works with his hands. My father wore a hard hat to protect his head on the work site. My mother wore an old canvas hat in the garden, beat up and beloved.

..

In her last days my mother would get out of bed for the gift of a cherry Danish, and that was a gift to me.

One of her last gifts was a bottle of argan oil for hair and for skin. Though it's now used up, I keep the empty bottle in the bathroom drawer. I tell myself there's still more in there, though I bang it into the palm of my hand, and nothing comes out.

Some days I long for her jaw-dropped silent judgement about what I paid for something, what I wore, how I thought, my indignation at the smallness of her attitudes, and my hunger for her acceptance. Other days I long for our shared outrage at the rudeness of some people and our despair for the unkindness of the world. These were our gifts to one another.

..

I returned the hat after the paddle in to Tsawout. My husband and I had to head home before the crew carried on to their Washington destination. Auntie Carrie thanked us for our help on road crew, and as we loaded the car and drove away, she sang a gratitude song. Another gift.

..

After a journey, it's customary for our canoe family, from *The Singing Coho*, to share those gifts we received from host communities. When they returned from the final events in Washington, I joined them for a gathering. It had only been a few days, but that energy between us was like the pull of the paddles, the cedar tree.

We drew names and handed out the gifts. There were several blankets and a drum, a drum bag and beaded jewelry. I was content to observe, but when all the gifts had been distributed, Auntie Carrie surprised me. "I want Judy to have this," she said, then presented me with the cedar hat. Her gift felt real, as if she'd first given it some consideration. This is how it should be.

I had no desire to run into the forest, to deny my deservedness. Holding the hat in my hand, I felt that I loved it because of who'd given it to me, and for its history. We'd experienced something important together. I'd earned this hat, and it had earned me. I thanked Auntie Carrie, who clearly wanted no fuss made, no ceremony. She motioned toward the elder who'd been on the journey with us and told me that it was she who had made it. I smiled at her and said thank-you, that it was beautiful. She nodded in silence.

..

Your stories come to you from your ancestors and are given to you as a gift, says Quw'utsun elder Harold Joe Sr. in the short documentary *Story of Cedar, Cedar Hat Weaving and Bark Pulling*. He goes on to say that an artist portrays his people through these stories and gives them back as another gift. I'm thinking of these words that I write here now as a gift to my family and to my grandchildren and to their grandchildren. Sometimes the memories and experiences from which I draw are gnarled scraps of cedar, but sometimes they're the light that turns the heartwood the colour gold.

# Readings

Writing this book has been a personal journey of truth and reconciliation with my Indigenous ancestral past and, at the same time, with my complicity in a colonialist system. Canadians are being called upon to do this work, and it's necessary we do it in a way that reflects who we are. Because I'm a writer and a reader, my path has involved reading and studying several books and other written sources. My work has been inspired by resources too numerous to list, however, the following reflects those that were most meaningful to me, and those directly consulted and referenced in *Permission to Land*.

All uses of the SENĆOŦEN language were sourced from the FirstVoices site: https://www.firstvoices.com/sencoten and from Dave Elliot Senior's *Saltwater People*. My apologies to the W̱SÁNEĆ (Saanich) people for any inaccuracies in my usage.

## Books

Research:

Leanne Betasamosake Simpson, *As We Have Always Done* (University of Minnesota Press, 2021)

Brenda J. Child, *Boarding School Seasons* (University of Nebraska Press, 1998)

Dave Elliott Sr., *Saltwater People* (Native Education, 1990)

Celia Haig-Brown, Garry Gottfriedson, Randy Fred, and the KIRS Survivors, *Tsqelmucwilc: The Kamloops Indian Residential School - Resistance and Reckoning* (Arsenal Pulp Press, 2022)

Daniel Heath Justice, *Why Indigenous Literatures Matter* (Wilfrid Laurier University Press, 2018)

Lee Maracle, *Celia's Song* (Cormorant Books, 2014)

Lee Maracle, *Memory Serves* (NeWest Press, 2015)

Lee Maracle, *My Conversations with Canadians* (Book*hug, 2017)

Christian W. McMillen, *Discovering Tuberculosis, A Global History, 1900 to the Present* (Yale University Press, 2015)

David Neel, *The Great Canoes: Reviving a Northwest Coast Tradition* (University of Washington Press, 1995)

David Wallace Adams, *Education for Extinction* (University Press of Kansas, 1995)

## Memoirs/Essays:

Jordan Abel, *NISHGA* (Penguin Random House, 2021)

Alicia Elliott, *A Mind Spread Out on the Ground* (Penguin Random House, 2019)

Danielle Geller, *Dog Flowers* (Penguin Random House, 2021)

Toni Jensen, *Carry: A Memoir of Survival on Stolen Land* (Ballantine Books, 2021)

Terese Marie Mailhot, *Heart Berries* (Penguin Random House, 2019)

Lorri Neilsen Glenn, *Following the River: Traces of Red River Women* (Wolsak & Wynn, 2017)

Susan Olding, *Pathologies: A Life in Essays* (Freehand Books, 2008)

## Poetry:

Louise B. Halfe, Sky Dancer, *Burning in This Midnight Dream* (Brick Books, 2021)

Philip Kevin Paul, *Little Hunger* (Harbour Publishing, 2008)

Philip Kevin Paul, *Taking the Names Down from the Hill* (Nightwood Editions, 2003)

Claudia Rankine, *Citizen: An American Lyric* (Graywolf Press, 2014)

## On Family Photography and Memory:

Roland Barthes, *Camera Lucida: Reflections on Photography* (1982)

Marianne Hirsch, *Family Frames: Photography, Narrative and Post-memory* (Harvard University Press, 1997)

Maria Stepanova, *In Memory of Memory* (New Directions, 2021)

## Online Reading:

Hilary Beaumont, "'Historical pattern of disregard': Inside one of the last remaining US Indigenous boarding schools" (*The Guardian*, 17 December 2022) www.theguardian.com/us-news/2022/dec/17/native-american-school-indigenous-students-suffered-future-hope

Liz Carter, "Renunciation #4" www.lizcarterartist.com/gallery?pgid=-joypv8uw-c6b5973f-f377-4fbe-b17a-6593504692c1

Edwin L. Chalcraft, *Assimilation's Agent: My Life as a Superintendent in the Indian Boarding School System* (University of Nebraska Press, 2004) muse.jhu.edu/book/11701

Chemawa Indian School, "History" (2015) chemawa.bie.edu/history.html

Comox Valley Art Gallery, "Potlatch 67–67: The Potlatch Ban—Then and Now: Liz Carter, Kwakwaka'wakw," *Ḥiłtsista'am* (*The Copper Will Be Fixed*) (2018) www.comoxvalleyartgallery.com/wp-content/uploads/mp/files/publications/files/takeaway-potlatch6767-w-artist-statements-web.pdf

Eduardo Duran, Bonnie Duran, Maria Yellow Horse Brave Heart, Susan Yellow Horse-Davis, "Healing the American Indian Soul Wound," *International Handbook of Multigenerational Legacies of Trauma* (Plenum Press, January 1998) www.researchgate.net/publication/232490895_Healing_the_American_Indian_Soul_Wound

Phil Ives & Louise McMurray, "Coast Salish Cedar Hat Weaving" (Independent Media Productions, 2012) www.youtube.com/watch?v=95rPwCDHOCE

Indian Residential Schools & Reconciliation, "1906–1910 The Bryce Report" (via the First Nations Education Steering Committee, 2015) www.fnesc.ca/wp/wp-content/uploads/2015/07/IRSR11-12-DE-1906-1910.pdf

Bryan Newland, "Federal Indian Boarding School Initiative Investigative Report" (Department of Indian Affairs, May 2022) www.bia.gov/sites/default/files/dup/inline-files/bsi_investigative_report_may_2022_508.pdf

Tŝilhqot'in Nation, "DADA NENTSEN GHA YATASTIG: I Am Going to Tell You About a Very Bad Disease. Tŝilhqot'in in the Time of COVID: Strengthening Tŝilhqot'in Ways to Protect Our People" (March 2021) www.tsilhqotin.ca/wp-content/uploads/2021/03/TNG-COVID-REPORT-FINAL.pdf

# Notes of Appreciation

Thank-you to the editors of the following magazines where these essays from the book appeared:

"Home Improvement (Great Grandparent's House)," *PRISM international*, Vancouver, BC, Issue 61.4

"Walking in the Wound," *Geist*, Vancouver, BC, Summer 2022

"Beneath the Din," *The Fiddlehead*, Fredericton, NB, Spring 2022

"Advice as Bread," *Prairie Fire*, Winnipeg, MB, Spring 2021

I'd like to acknowledge my mother, Rose LeBlanc, who, with my father, gave me life. I hope that were she still alive she would see this book as the tribute it is to her strength and her beauty both inside and out. I'd like to thank my father, Alphonse LeBlanc, for rising to the difficult conversations and being able to say, "It is the truth." Thank-you to my sister Teri for her ongoing love and support and to my brother Allan for sharing his memories. I'd also like to thank my Auntie Faye who never tires of telling family stories. Her honesty and humour have done much to ease this sometimes difficult work. Thanks to Uncle Sonny for his photos and his family stories. Thank-you to Lisa Peppan for her extensive research into the Houston/Bartleman family and for those hours we wiled away in that restaurant in Tacoma talking all things family. I want to express my deepest appreciation to Brenda Bartleman for making space for me and all my questions in her life, calling me "Cousin" and welcoming me into the ZIȻOT family. And thank-you to Judy Bartleman for sketching a family tree for me during that visit to her home so many years ago. Thanks to Philip Kevin Paul for the history he shared with me about Senanus Island and for his beautiful poetry.

With a full heart, I want to express my deepest and warmest gratitude for Carrie Reid, Jessie Recalma and all the members of the Singing Coho Canoe Family for opening up a whole new world to me. Thanks, especially, to Carrie for her kindness, wisdom and generosity, and for reading the section of the book about Tribal Journeys before publication.

I also want to acknowledge the Seattle archives for the digital documents they shared with me during the COVID lockdown from Chemawa Indian School and for their assistance when I was finally able to continue my research on site in 2022. Thank-you to Kevin Loftus from the San Juan Historical Museum and to their researcher, Robin, who sent me an envelope stuffed with information about my great-grandparents' lives on San Juan Island.

I don't know where I'd be without my writing community. Thank-you, especially, to Cornelia Hoogland for suggesting the title of this book, and for reading my early efforts while offering her insights, encouragement and constant friendship. Thanks to Ted Hoogland for a beta read and a fruitful conversation about the direction I might take in the writing of the book. Thanks to my 4 Sages writing group (Troni, Sheryl, and Joan) for their thoughtful readings from sections of the book. I'd like to acknowledge Arleen Paré and Frances Backhouse for their feedback on "Walking in the Wound," and for their faithful friendship. My appreciation to Lorri Neilsen Glenn who was my instructor at the Sage Hill writing retreat and offered me valuable feedback on the project and specifically on "Place of Rupture." And huge appreciation to Susan Olding for her astute understanding of my vision for the manuscript, and her wise feedback after reading a complete draft.

Thank-you to Vici Johnstone, Sarah Corsie, Malaika Aleba and Pam Robertson at Caitlin Press for believing in this book and for their attentive work in getting it to publication.

And Brian Latta, thank-you for being the one who rode the often difficult and emotional seas with me during this long exploration. You are my safe harbour.

# About the Author

PHOTO BRIAN LATTA

Judy LeBlanc is a writer from Fanny Bay, BC. Several of her stories and essays have been published in Canadian literary journals; a collection of her short stories, *The Promise of Water*, was published by Oolichan Books in 2017, and her novel, *The Broken Heart of Winter*, was published by Caitlin Press in 2023. She won the Sheldon Currie Fiction Prize in 2012, the Islands Fiction Contest in 2015, and she's been a runner-up for fiction contests held by *Room*, *PRISM international* and the CBC. She was born and raised on the West Coast. She has Acadian ancestry on her father's side and European/W̱SÁNEĆ ancestry on her mother's side. She was the founder of the Fat Oyster Reading Series in Fanny Bay and taught creative writing at North Island College for several years.